Gillian Grayson

FORGOTTEN

AUSTIN MACAULEY PUBLISHERS™

LONDON • CAMBRIDGE • NEW YORK • SHARJAH

Ordering Information
Quantity sales: Special discounts are available on quantity purchases by corporations, associations, and others. For details, contact the publisher at the address below.

Publisher's Cataloging-in-Publication data
Grayson, Gillian
Forgotten

ISBN 9781685622459 (Paperback)
ISBN 9781685622466 (Hardback)
ISBN 9781685622473 (ePub e-book)

Library of Congress Control Number: 2023904497

www.austinmacauley.com/us

First Published 2023
Austin Macauley Publishers LLC
40 Wall Street, 33rd Floor, Suite 3302
New York, NY 10005
USA

mail-usa@austinmacauley.com
+1 (646) 5125767

Table of Contents

Dedication

I wish to dedicate this book to my Heavenly Father, who was my counselor and guided me through The Nightmare Years, giving me the strength, the courage, the perseverance, and the knowledge that I so badly needed in order to deal with so much pain and tragedy, thereby allowing me to break the bonds of silence and bravely and truthfully tell my story.

"For it is by grace you have been saved, through faith – and this is not from yourselves, it is a gift from God."

–Ephesians 2:8

Acknowledgement

There are some very special individuals who were placed in my life at very important times, and I wish to sincerely thank them. I could not have finished this book without their support and their help.

To my daughter, who was always there for me, providing the help and support that others should have been giving to me during The Nightmare Years. So sadly, she did not survive those terrible stormy years, but I'm sure she has a special place in heaven. She was such a very special gift to me.

To my son, who has also suffered from some of the aftermaths of what happened during The Nightmare Years but who has always hung in there for me. I am so thankful to him for being part of my life. He has been such a tremendous gift to me.

To my son, his wife, and their two children who believed me and in me when I shared part of my story with them. I feel truly blessed to have them in my life. I'm so grateful to them and for them.

To a good friend, who also believed me and in me, and who read one of the last drafts of this book and gave me her honest feedback. Thank you, friend.

To that incredible social worker, who believed me and in me, who was always steadfast in her support of me when I had no other support, and who had tremendous insight into my life. I also thank her for reading the second last draft of this book, critiquing it, and providing her professional opinion.

To the wonderful care manager, who always had faith in me, who always supported me, and who had a greater insight into my life than I realized at the time.

To that amazing man, who came into my life in 2008, who always believed me and in me, who has helped me to build my new life, who has been such a positive influence in my life, and who put up with me while I was writing this book.

To that wonderful friend, who, knowing about my very limited computer skills, had the kindness and the patience to teach me everything I needed to know in order to write my story.

To the Production Coordinators and all others at Austin Macauley Publishers who assisted in bringing this book to publication. I sincerely thank you for your help, your guidance, and your patience.

I extend my heartfelt thanks to all of you.

Prologue

Years ago, a friend and I went for a walk around our acreage subdivision. She told me about a book entitled *When Rabbit Howls* by Truddi Chase. We decided to read the book.

My friend was a very intelligent person, but she was totally baffled by what the book entailed. I was not. I seemed to understand it quite clearly, and that really surprised me. It's an incredibly sordid story about an individual's life that was so negatively impacted by horrific sexual, emotional, and physical abuses and acts of violence against her that are dehumanizing, degrading, disgusting, and almost unbelievable. Why would I understand why Truddi needed to escape from herself? I shouldn't have been able to understand.

If I'd known that reading the book at that particular time in my life would be a part of what would, in a relatively short time, cause such destruction in my life and cause such heartache and pain, I would certainly not have read it. Another much more crucial part of my destructed life was being a member of a church with secrets, also at that time. Those two things set in motion the beginning of a long and horrible journey that I would take during the next years.

Now I have my own story to tell that is full of so much pain, torment, and crazymaking, leaving me with more loss than anyone should have to bear, leaving me with issues surrounding my childhood that no child should ever have to look after and deal with, and dealing with multiple issues in the rest of my life that came at me so fast – all of which stole my life away.

Never ever in my wildest dreams would I ever have thought that I would be writing a book, and certainly not a book like this one, but there were a few horrendous years in my life when having just the right book at just the right time saved my sanity for sure, and possibly my life. I discovered how extremely important a book can be. It is my prayer that my story will bring more understanding about what severe damages abuse can do to an individual.

I also pray that this book reaches someone who really needs to hear that they are not alone and that someone understands.

Writing this book was one of the hardest things I've ever had to do, and I have done it with some very mixed feelings. I hope that, as this story is read, the reader will keep an open mind.

Chapter 1
Secrecy and Silence

My story begins at a church where I had been a member of the congregation for fourteen or fifteen years. I had not grown up in a church atmosphere and had never been a member of any church previously, so becoming a member had been a very big step for me. It had taken me a long time to settle into church life, but my children had decided that they wished to begin attending a church, and I was certainly not going to deny them that wish. I thought I was in a safe place at the church, although I always sat in the back row on the end seat, ready for an escape. At the time, I didn't know why. It had taken me several years to trust in the church. Churches are supposed to be safe places – right? Eventually, I felt comfortable enough to start up a few drama groups, and we had a lot of fun for several years. I thought that I had found myself a really nice church family, and I took great delight in that. I became a very loyal and committed member of that church.

Then, in 1992, things changed. The church became a tense place to be. Mistrust was building amongst the congregation. There was minimal laughter now, and it wasn't the happy place it once used to be. I would walk into a room, and the people who'd been having a conversation would see me and stop talking. I sometimes thought they were talking about me. So many people were upset. I knew that something was going on that I/we didn't know about, but we were supposedly what they called a "family," and good families don't keep bad secrets, do they? The word sinister comes to mind because I was beginning to feel really uncomfortable in this church. I did not feel safe there anymore. When had I felt like this before and when had I seen all of this before? I was having some very unsettling feelings deep within me, and I was getting some terrible knots in my stomach.

And so, the secrecy and silence of spiritual abuse, at its very finest, began. Oh, I didn't recognize it as that at the time, but I learned about it very quickly. I learned about it the hard way. The 'don't talk and don't tell' rule came into effect, and the big coverup began – that 'no talk' rule which always happens in incestuous emotional and incestuous sexual abusive homes, the toying of peoples' feelings, nobody knowing what was going on, becoming suspicious of others, not knowing who to trust anymore, and not being told what is going on – just like the typical dysfunctional toxic families with secrets to hide. We were all affected in some way or other, but for me? For me, my walk through hell began. I will always refer to the following 10 to 15 years as *The Nightmare Years*. I was a prime candidate for repressed memory recovery (RMR) of childhood abuse which left me open to, and ripe for, further abuse (which will become clear later). I would be very remiss if I didn't give this church full marks for triggering the memories I had hidden in my mind for so long – memories that were much too painful for me to remember earlier in my life and were soon going to send me into terrible emotional pain that, in a very short time, left me in such anguish that I could barely endure it – memories that were buried so very deeply within me and had been hidden in my subconscious for very good reasons. I did 'not' want them brutally dug out! The following is an account of how this all came to be.

****

As all that craziness at the church was unfolding, and also in 1992, I had taken on the task of being guardian and trustee for both of my parents. My father had multiple TIA's (mini-strokes) beginning on 1st August 1992, and he and my mother (after many meetings and some intense explaining about my parent's life together) were both placed in a nursing home at that time.

Taking on the task of being a guardian for my parents was a monumental task. They were not the average set of parents. They'd always fought loudly and constantly. My mother was very slow mentally, and my father had always cared for her. I was about to learn and to realize what a difficult and frustrating job that had been for him and was now going to be for me. When I first tried to find a place for my parents to live, I had tried to get them into the lodge in the town of Sherville, but I was shocked to learn that they would not accept my parents as residents. A few years before, my father's first TIA's, they had lived at the lodge, but they had been asked to leave because of all the fighting, yelling, and disruption they had caused there. I had never been told about that. I was stunned to hear about it, and that was the first of many shocks I was soon to receive.

It was obvious why my father required nursing care, as his left side had been left very impaired by a series of TIA's, and his thought processes were very affected as well. He relied very heavily on me for all of the decision-making. It was an entirely different story in my mother's case. It was really hard to get her into that first nursing home. She had always functioned at a very low level, and it took some serious meetings with some professionals before they gained insight into who she really was. The social worker I was working with found it inconceivable that she required nursing care since she and my father had been married for so long – fifty years. They just couldn't believe it at first. All things appeared so normal and average as far as they could see. And, it became clear very quickly that my sister and her husband (Jean and Ed) were going to be a huge hindrance to me in my endeavor to clarify the facts surrounding our parents. On the day my father had his first strokes, my sister, her husband, my mother and I met with his doctor. The doctor asked us if my father had been under any stress. My brother-in-law quickly replied, "No." Well, that was just plain ridiculous! I was shocked at his answer and could hardly believe he'd said that. I immediately said, "Yes, a lot of stress for a long time." It was way past time for some truth-telling. This was going to cause a total, but very needed, break in the family.

I just could not believe how Jean and Ed could totally dismiss the reality of our parents' lives. It seemed like they tried to make it appear as if we were all just a regular, normal family, and there wasn't much wrong with my mother. To be fair, our parents knew how to put on quite the display. When we had company, it appeared as if things were just fine. My mother could be so loving – much too loving at times. I think most people could see that she had mental health issues. Why try to keep something that was so obvious a secret when it was so easy to see? But Jean and Ed tried to do just that. Cover it up. Pretend everything is just great. Some years before, Ed had said that "If you tell someone something, whether it's right or wrong, you don't ever change your story, even if you find out later on that it isn't true." Needless to say, it is very difficult to deal with people like him and also like Jean, who both have all the signs of very closed minds. During the next years, they would cause a great deal of trouble for my mother and even more for me with their complete denial of how things were with our parents.

****

My father had taken my mother over to Jean and Ed's home about a year before he'd had the strokes. He had told them that he couldn't deal with her anymore. He was well into his seventies, and he wanted to find a place for her to live separately from him – a group home, perhaps, where there were people similar to her that she could relate to and where she could live happily. He wanted to spend his last days in peace. He had lived with this wife who caused nothing but disruption and frustration for all those years, and he couldn't do it anymore. It was too hard on him, and his health was beginning to fail. He wanted the support of his children. Jean and Ed, apparently, implied that he was being ridiculous, that there wasn't much wrong with her and he was the problem. They told my parents to leave their house. Much later, when I tried to discuss this with Jean, she just replied, "One is as bad as the other." Cover it up. Sweep it under the rug. And I was in the horrible position of looking after the end results.

My father came to me for help shortly after that. He was a desperate man. It was rather heartless that Jean and Ed had offered him no help nor understanding. It had never been hard for me to see that my mother was not of high intelligence, so I readily agreed that she should be tested. This should have been done many years ago. I located a hospital in the city near where I lived (Cedar City) that would do that. Luckily, my father and I had her tested at that hospital, so I had the paperwork explaining her low mental ability and her inability to function as an average individual – poor decision-making, inability to comprehend simple matters, etc.

****

That paperwork is what finally got her into the nursing home. They admitted her conditionally because of that assessment, but they didn't think she really needed to be there. After she'd been there a short while though, the staff began to see that she really did need to be there. She behaved herself for a while. She had always been capable of making people believe that she was

14

of average intelligence and socially adept – sometimes for as long as a month or so. After several months, the staff could no longer deal with her rages, her demands, her lack of decision-making and comprehension, and her personality and behavior disorders. She couldn't get along with anyone for very long. She was so disruptive, everyone around her was negatively affected, and they arranged for her to go to the Sherville Psychiatric Hospital for assessment and diagnosis. And the crazy-making that was to go on for the next years had begun.

When I met with a room full of psychiatrists and other staff at the Psychiatric Hospital, they were astonished at the story of my parents. One of the psychiatrists remarked on what *a fascinating story this is*. Well, let me tell you that if you've had to live within that story, it is not fascinating. It is tragic. They had done a lot of tests during the assessment, and it was at this time that they informed me, amongst other things, that my mother was borderline mentally handicapped.

This was a terrible shock that impacted me horribly. Some years before, my father had tried to tell one of his sisters (my aunt) about my mother's behaviors and lack of intelligence. She had just told him, "Well, we all forget things sometimes." When I told that same aunt, at this time, that my mother was borderline mentally handicapped, all she said was that it's amazing my sister and I were OK. My God. While I always knew that my mother was slow, I had not even considered her being mentally handicapped. What did that make me? I had read somewhere that the normal and bright children of mentally handicapped parents are statistically a small group but are at serious risk for adjustment problems. Half of the study group of mentally handicapped parents had negative adaptations. One-fourth of the group took on the parental role, and one-fourth showed average adjustment.

I was to learn that I had taken on the parental role. My sister? Well, she just pretended that everything was just fine, so I don't know which category she would fall into. Is it possible that Jean didn't/couldn't face the reality? Didn't have the insight to understand? Or did she simply choose to just deny it all because it was too embarrassing? I must say, though, that when you tell anyone that your mother is mentally handicapped, they do look at you differently. I suppose they wonder how handicapped you are as well. It is a terrible thing to have to live with. My mother was embarrassing, and it was often humiliating to have to deal with her. We didn't put ourselves into that position, but we still have had to live with it. It is our reality, and it is a tough reality.

****

I will never forget walking through the doors of the Psychiatric Hospital for the first time, and I must comment on it. I never dreamt that I would ever be walking the halls of a psychiatric facility. Although I have some nursing training, I knew very little about mental health, little about what abuse can do to an individual, and very little about how to deal with those affected by abuse or any type of mental illness. I found it very eerie and very frightening. I was extremely tense as I walked past individuals with vacant, staring eyes, other individuals who carried on continuous conversations with themselves, and others who appeared to glare at me with what felt like hate, mistrust, or fear. I felt deep sorrow for all of them.

****

While my mother was in the Psychiatric Hospital, my father required surgery for an AAA Repair. He had a final massive stroke following the surgery and died sixteen days later on 3 February/94. Because my father had died, my mother was sent back from the Sherville Psychiatric Hospital to the nursing home without a full assessment having been done. The last few years had been really hard on me with helping my father through the last 1½ years of his life, taking him to the necessary hospitals, meeting all the demands of my mother, dealing with the staff and her with regard to all the problems she was causing, going back and forth to the Psychiatric Hospital (all the meetings with the psychiatrists and making the explanations over and over again), paying all of the bills, doing all of her personal shopping, driving back and forth to my home which was 2 ½ hours away from the nursing home, arranging my father's funeral, and fending off irate relatives who couldn't understand the nightmarish steps I was taking with my mother and couldn't see why someone like her should have to go to a Psychiatric Hospital. It was suddenly all my fault that she was there.

Before the funeral, I had phoned Jean, told her about all of the arrangements I had made, and asked for her feedback. Some support would

16

have been nice, but I really didn't expect it and certainly didn't get it. Actually, my father and I had discussed what he wanted for his funeral, and I just carried through with his requests. Jean's only problem had been with one of the pallbearers, whom she said was a drunk in Sherville. It would embarrass them. I took him off the pallbearer's list, even though my father had requested him. Later on, Jean and Ed implied that they knew nothing about what was to happen at the funeral, and that is what they told the relatives. Yet my daughter had been next to me listening to that phone call. Why was it that they were so insistent on misinterpreting the facts? To make me look bad amongst the relatives? Couldn't she remember that phone call from me? It made no sense.

I had a husband, a 21-year-old daughter, and a 16-year-old son at home, and my children needed me, but I was so busy dealing with all of the issues that constantly kept coming at me, and I was getting so worn down. My poor children. I talked to them about their grandpa's death and gave each of them a really good book on death and dying and about the mourning and grieving process. At that time, I trusted my husband to take care of things at home while I looked after all of the issues surrounding my parents' situations and got everything in order. Little did I know...

****

It was toward the end of February '94 when this fellow (Grant) that my daughter was seeing came to me. I had only heard a little about him – his name and little else. I didn't know him at all. She'd only brought him home for us to meet him once or twice. Grant reeked of liquor both times and didn't make any sense to me whatsoever. He didn't seem to be very intelligent. I had hoped that this was just another boyfriend who would come and go as the others had. (I had been so proud when my daughter had begun college in the fall of '93, and I looked forward to her completing the two-year program).

I was absolutely stunned when Grant said that he wanted to get married to my daughter. Oh, how I tried to talk him out of that. I knew it would be a horrible mistake and a disaster, especially at this time. This couldn't be happening! I told him I had way too much on my plate right now. I was wrung out. There was way too much happening in my family – my father had just died, my mother was way out-of-control, I had so much to look after, the church was in a mess, I was so traumatized, and I went on and on. This was

17

not a good time for a wedding! He just ignored everything I said. My God, this was not good timing! My daughter (Kayla) had suffered terrible bullying from a group of girls in high school. I'd just helped her through that a few years before. She was still healing from that time, and she had just recently lost her "funny grandpa" (as my children had always called him). She was now watching her mother dealing with all of this crisis and watching her father do absolutely nothing to help. She was also watching her grandmother going into a Psychiatric Hospital – a very scary thing for a young person.

We were a family very quickly going into crisis. Kayla was so very vulnerable, and that is when a guy like Grant can take advantage of that vulnerability. I couldn't reason with Grant at all. He literally took power and control over Kayla and her life at the very worst time in our lives.

****

Finally, in April '94, I made the arrangement for my mother to be transferred to a nursing home in Cedar City. She was getting into more and more trouble at the nursing home in Sherville, and I thought it would be easier for me to deal with all of her issues if she lived closer to my home. Jean had, apparently, gone to her angry and wondering why she was going to move to Cedar City. I've often wondered at her reasoning. Very strange, under all of the circumstances.

If I'd known how tough it was going to be for me in the near future, I would have left her in Sherville, but I was her guardian and I took that responsibility very seriously. I had asked Jean to become an alternate guardian, and she had said, "No." She had given me all kinds of lame excuses as to why she wouldn't agree to be an alternate. She had lived in the same house as I had growing up and had lived in the same town as our parents for many years. There were probably numerous embarrassing times when our parents had fought in public and when my father showed his temper, or when my mother had said some really ridiculous things in response to inquiries or within various conversations. She could never get the stories straight, and what came out of her mouth was sometimes so ridiculous, so wrong, and so farfetched. You'd think my sister would have been happy (and relieved) to see her mother move away from Sherville. Strange. It didn't make any sense to me at all. I do remember her saying, "We have to live in Sherville." I can only assume that the point of her statement was that she didn't want her parents' story out there for everyone to know about. It would be "too embarrassing" – (her words). Did she not realize that some people could see what her parents were like? So why wouldn't she be happy about this move? Jean and Ed just pretended that all was well and that there was nothing much wrong with our mother. Cover it up. This was all so ridiculous. They were both people who always had to be right, and they didn't like it when they were beginning to be proven wrong, time and time again. At any rate, they could not be relied on for help at all.

****

It's interesting to note here that my sister was/is very much like our mother in many ways. She tells stories that are not quite true, just embellishing the stories enough to make them more 'interesting' just like our mother. She has the same demanding personality and always has to be right. She is not mentally challenged. I believe she's had demons of her own to deal with (outstanding from her childhood) that make her seek that extra attention. When she was nineteen, she married a man who was fifteen years older than she was – a father figure? Maybe. Ed is a very controlling figure, and Jean just falls in line with him. In at least one way, they are a good match because they both like to embellish the truth, and they both have to be right all the time. It has been exceedingly difficult – actually impossible – to deal with either one of them. They certainly caused a lot of damage to my life as a result of their denial and fabrication of facts concerning what was really going on in our mother's life.

****

I moved my mother to Cedar City. I was called into the new nursing home almost daily to look after whatever problem she had, and there were many. She couldn't get along with the staff or the residents there, she would throw chairs around in anger and upset all the residents (who became very frightened of her), and she would have outburst after outburst. They relied on me to calm her and to explain things to her over and over and over again. At one point, they threatened to call the police, as they were so afraid that she was going to hurt someone. She could have been charged with assault. She'd just ignite out of the blue and would shout at whoever was nearby. When she was taken away from a bad situation, she would pout in her room for hours. She was also in the mourning process, and that was really tough because she was of such a low IQ and didn't understand the mourning and grieving process.

About three months later, she was placed in a different nursing home where she caused even more disruption – pushing residents in wheelchairs into walls, pushing and shoving residents and staff, shouting at the staff and residents, and demanding, demanding, and demanding in a terrible rage. I was under enormous stress, and I was so exhausted. She was a very complicated human being. I was becoming so traumatized by all of these issues and demands that confronted me so quickly. I had moved out of my birth home the minute I turned sixteen and had forgotten my childhood. I was soon to learn that I'd done that in order to survive.

****

In the midst of all this, my daughter and this guy insisted on getting married. There was no talking either one of them out of this marriage. I had gone to my minister and asked him for help for my daughter. He'd met with my daughter and Grant only once, and he'd simply dismissed them. His only response to me was "They're living together anyway, and there's nothing I can do." What kind of a minister was this guy that I had so entrusted my faith with anyway? Was my daughter of no importance? I didn't know then that this minister was in a lot of trouble at the church, and the church was keeping it all under wraps and not telling the congregants (the church family) what was happening in 'our' church.

I asked my husband for help, and he just ignored it all. In my very traumatized state of mind, I eventually concluded that what I thought I was seeing with my daughter and this guy couldn't be as bad as it really was. It just couldn't be that bad – not right now! And, in a daze, I was sewing Kayla's wedding dress, two bridesmaid dresses, and a dress for myself. I was also organizing a wedding.

It couldn't be that bad? Well, how wrong I was. I was to find out very soon that it was much worse than I'd thought. We went through with the wedding. Big mistake. Horrible mistake. At the wedding, I drew aside my new son-in-law's co-worker and asked, "What is it with Grant? He doesn't make any sense to me." His response was, "Grant is trouble. Boy, are you people in for it." He and I met later on, and he explained that statement to me.

I was astonished and shocked at what he told me. Grant would always get to work late and was often drunk and reeked of liquor at work. He'd had drinking and drug issues since high school. He was 29 years old at this time, and I wondered why his family had not ever intervened for him. Obviously, they had not. They'd certainly had plenty of time to do so. He had no business sense and was unable to communicate with people properly because he couldn't carry on a sensible conversation. Therefore, he couldn't deal with any customers. He always went to work dirty, grubby, and unkempt. It was very embarrassing for the other staff, and the employees had no respect for him. He couldn't do any books. All he was capable of doing was using the business machines. He couldn't deal with the public, look after prospective customers, or do any of the 'business end' of things, for obvious reasons. Grant's father had passed his half of the machine business down to him. Otherwise, he never would have been hired on there. Grant's father had recently retired. Grant got half of the business, his two sisters got a cash settlement, and the three of them were fighting. The sisters were claiming that Grant got more money than they did. I was to learn that because Grant's parents and the co-worker's parents were friends, the co-worker didn't wish to become further involved in anything further, and he asked me to keep this meeting between only him and me. I respected his wishes. I sure did appreciate the information he passed along to me, though. I could foresee a very rough road ahead of me. My God, what a mess my daughter had landed in. And I was already dealing with so many other harsh issues that just kept flying at me.

The day after the wedding, I sat in a lawn chair in our backyard, looking at my flower garden. What a horrible mistake this wedding had been. If I hadn't been under so much duress for so long with all this craziness surrounding me, I would have seen this coming. Damn it! I should have seen this coming! Under normal circumstances, I never would have let Kayla marry a guy like Grant – never in a million years. I would have fought it tooth and nail! My circumstances were not normal then! As a social worker once told me, I was a victim of horrendous circumstances – so was my daughter.

As I sat in my backyard, I wept...and I wept...

I told my husband (Joe) what I had learned and tried to get him to help me deal with Kayla's situation. All he did was look at me and say, "Well, she got herself into it." Later on, he saw the drunken parties – all the drinking, swearing, and craziness. Where was my beautiful daughter? I didn't recognize her amongst that drunken group of people. This wasn't the daughter I knew at all. She didn't belong there. I was shocked at what I was seeing and how she had changed. Joe saw her being pushed and shoved by this guy, and he did nothing. Over and over, I asked Joe for help, with no result whatsoever. When I drew attention to the drunkenness, the drugs that were talked about (Grant openly admitted that he took drugs), and the fact that we now saw our daughter drinking heavily and being treated very badly, he just repeated, "Well, she got herself into it." He didn't do one damned thing to help her! How can a father sit back and watch something like that?

And, it got worse. At one of the first gatherings with Grant and his family, Grant's mother said she only had one good child out of three. Grant was not 'the good one'. She proceeded to use that famous 'F' word as if it was just a common word – using it five times in one sentence. It was astounding. One sister seemed to have her life together (the good child), although I will always wonder why she hadn't intervened for her alcoholic brother. She and her family had had many years to do so. The other sister was obviously an anorexic and had lived with numerous different men – three within the past four years. She treated Kayla pretty viciously and accused Kayla of marrying Grant for his money. My God! Grant was obviously an alcoholic. [In the 4 1/2 years I knew him, I never did have a decent conversation with him. It is impossible to deal with a drunk – a guy who has absolutely no insight and who can't get stories straight (very much like my mother)]. The three children were fighting over their parents' money, and it went on and on – a thoroughly dysfunctional family. And, with what I was dealing with in my personal life, they were the last people I should have been anywhere near.

I knew I had to intervene for Kayla. I couldn't leave her in that mess. Joe was aware of all of the above. He should have been helping me to intervene for his daughter. Even in the delicate state of health I was now in, I could easily see that Kayla was in serious trouble in that marriage, but by this time I could barely drag myself through the day. I pleaded with Joe to help us. But he didn't.

Chapter 2
Buried Memories

In the meantime, at the church, the minister was suddenly gone, and an interim minister was there now. Why? I went to a church meeting in September 1994. I had a question about the drama group, and I intended to stay for the entire meeting. Foolishly, I thought I might be able to be of some help, as I was very concerned about what was going on at the church. It wasn't a very healthy place for me to be at this time in my life when I was dealing with such horrendous issues in my personal life. When I was done making my request for the drama group, I sat back and was ready to stay for the rest of the meeting. I was just stunned when the chairperson told me in a very stern, hurtful manner to leave the meeting. We had always been told that these were open meetings!

It felt like I had been kicked out because they had things to discuss that I was not supposed to hear, and even though I was supposed to be part of that church family, I definitely was not to be included in any family decision-making. I was shocked that they kicked me out. I was beginning to associate this so-called church family with the family I had been a part of for the first sixteen years of my life, and it was not at all good.

About three days after I was kicked out of the church meeting, I began to have memories of my childhood resurfacing. They were like a movie that I was watching, and I actually lived through the memories. What I was remembering stopped me in my tracks. They were not good memories. I didn't know what was happening to me. I thought that maybe this was delayed mourning. I had not cried after my father's death. So many hard issues were coming at me way too quickly. I couldn't catch up, and I had no help or support at all, although I had repeatedly asked for it.

In October or November, I went on a trip to Florida with my husband. I couldn't remember the flight there, nor back. I had always been the map-reader, yet I couldn't make any sense of the map I had in front of me. The words were all out of focus, and it was all blurry. I couldn't believe it! At night, I kept getting up because these memories (which I later learned were called flashbacks) were coming into my mind so hard and fast, slamming into my mind so quickly. I couldn't do anything about it. I couldn't stop them. And oh, how I wanted this remembering to stop! My husband just ignored it all and went to sleep. And what I have always referred to as *The Nightmare Years* had begun in full force.

****

My church was a really bad place for me to be at this time. I was now experiencing intense pain throughout my body. I thought it was because of all the severe and prolonged stress I was under. Somehow, in the terrible state of health I was in, I did direct what was to be my last drama presentation at the church around the end of February '95. I could see that the drama group was concerned about me. I could no longer concentrate on what to do nor how to direct the group. I had to write all the directions down on paper during the day and try to read them to the cast during rehearsals. They couldn't have imagined what was happening in my personal life or to me. I really didn't know the full extent of it myself.

I only went back to the church once after the last performances. I sat in a pew, trying to get all the things that were happening to me and around me into perspective. I needed to try to make sense of all the craziness and crazy-making surrounding me. I couldn't believe all of these things were happening to me. I couldn't believe that my health was failing so rapidly. I'd always been so healthy. Everything was happening way too fast. I didn't know what was happening to me, and I couldn't believe that my husband was doing – you guessed it – nothing. He had simply watched me, for months now, in this frail state – in terrible pain throughout my body, unable to remember things, unable to know what to say unless I wrote it down and read it. I didn't know then how deeply traumatized I was and how deeply I was going into shock. And these damn memories kept slamming into my mind. My head was a mass of pain. Oh God, what's happening to me? Why was my husband not seeking medical help for me?

One should be able to find some peace or solace in a church. I was in that church for a very short time because I became ice-cold. I had not felt such evil as I felt at that time, and I never want to feel that evilness ever again. I got out of there as quickly as I could and never went back to that horrible place. [I was soon going to recognize that what had been taking place in that church was spiritual abuse. I didn't know then that it was going to take a great many years before I could even bring myself to step into any church anywhere after what this one was so instrumental in doing to me. Spiritual abuse is brutal.]

****

I couldn't think straight anymore. The memories were slamming into my mind so quickly and so fiercely now. I couldn't speak much anymore, I stuttered for the first time in my life, and I was beginning to experience terrible physical pain. Joe did nothing. A responsible husband would have been taking me to doctors or, at the very least, comforting me, supporting me, or – doing something! He should have been talking to his daughter about what was going on. But not Joe! There had been so many red flags concerning Grant, and Joe had just ignored them. He did what he'd always done best – nothing. He simply went on with his life as if nothing important was happening in our family. Unbelievable. As the days went by, I was slipping into deeper and deeper shock as these memories slammed into my mind, and I was in such physical and emotional pain that I was barely able to get through the day. In the terrible state of health I was in, I couldn't help my daughter. That will always haunt me.

****

I'd 'forgotten' about my mother's behaviors. She had now turned into a wild woman. She telephoned me at least twenty times a day – all yelling and screaming. I didn't think she knew how to use a phone. Maybe she had talked one of the staff into dialing my number for her. She was extremely demanding of the staff and of me. There came a time when my health started failing even more quickly, and I couldn't take those calls anymore. I was way, way beyond being over-extended. I changed our phone number. She had no concept of what the yelling and screaming and all the complaining she was yelling at me was doing to me. The director of the home said that she set the tone for the entire building, and all the residents would be upset, which, as you can well imagine, caused multiple problems for the staff. Almost everyone was afraid of her. She also said that my mother was always much worse when she was around men. That would be an important disclosure in time to come. She had become very violent. It was a horror scene.

Jean and Ed would go to see our mother once in a while. Every single time after they left, she was so upset and disruptive that I was called in to calm her. They didn't seem to have the insight to say things that didn't upset her. I began to think that they might have to be told not to go to see her. Their visits just caused more problems, and there were plenty of problems already. The staff and I did not need more.

The director and nursing staff at the nursing home had become very concerned about me. They thought I was having an emotional breakdown. They kept asking me, "Where is your husband?" They could see my mental and physical health deteriorating so quickly. They hadn't experienced anyone quite like my mother before. She was way, way out-of-control. She was like a tornado, hurricane, earthquake, and tsunami. I had been constantly called in to help as it seemed that I was the only one who could calm her for a bit. My stress level was way off the charts. Nursing homes, doctors, my daughter, others were all concerned about me. Why wasn't my husband seeing this, helping me, and doing something about any of these issues? Why wasn't he helping his daughter? Why was he ignoring the horrible state of my health? Why wasn't he seeing what so many others could plainly see? I kept hoping that, at some point, his mind would open, and he would see what was going on right in front of him. Instead, he minimized and denigrated everything I told him and just didn't 'see' any of it. Even today, I still cannot believe his nonchalance regarding the crisis his family was in. I was barely functioning. My life was going past me in a blur of flashbacks, and I was floundering in a world filled with such physical and emotional pain that I still can't even begin to describe. All I could do was keep trying to just hang in there. How could he be that blind?

Finally, the nursing staff had to give my mother an injection to calm her, and it took five strong staff members (she was a very large woman) to restrain her to her bed – a strait jacket. They made arrangements for her to be transferred by ambulance to the Cedar City Psychiatric Hospital, where they did more assessing, tried different medications, and she was seen by psychiatrists. She remained at the hospital for about six months. I went there a few times, but I just couldn't go anymore. I shouldn't have been driving in the state I was in. I was just in too much physical pain and in the midst of too much mental turmoil. I couldn't think straight anymore as those damn memories just kept coming into my mind at a faster and faster pace.

I learned that psychiatrists who deal with those states of mental health every day (like my mother's mental state with all of that anger and rage) need to do some self-counseling. The high energy level is so intense, and I discovered from personal experience that it is 'catchy'. The immense energy high emitted by the transference of energy from individuals like my mother is enormous. It's exhausting. One has to escape for a time to refresh the mind so that the mind is calm and clear once more. After dealing with a mother like mine, I now understand this. Believe me I have tremendous respect for doctors, nurses, and all staff who work with the mentally ill every day. They are amazing individuals who deal with such unpredictability and harshness so much of the time – an extremely stressful job.

****

The world around me was a crazy place. How could so many terrible issues be coming at me all at the same time? Everything was so terribly out of place in my life. Why wasn't Joe helping with some of this? How is it that he couldn't see what was happening to me – to his daughter – to my mother? What the hell was wrong with him? I was begging him for help, and I was getting more and more desperate as the days went by. I tried so hard to explain to some relatives what was going on with my mother. They didn't believe how bad the situation really was, and when I tried so hard to tell Jean about her mother's antics, she just said, "Oh, it isn't that bad." Jean should have been helping, but she just acted like nothing much was going on, and her mother was fine. She just denied everything and pretended that 'nothing much is happening'. Trying to get Jean to understand was just plain futile and a waste of my time. Nobody believed me. I got no help or support from anyone.

****

I was experiencing severe pain throughout my body. I had been under horrendous, bad stress for so long, not being believed and not getting any help. The pain had begun in my neck and shoulders, but it was now invading my entire body. There was extreme pain in the tissues and muscles throughout my body – neck, shoulders, elbows, wrists, buttocks, hips, thighs, legs, knees, ankles, feet, chest wall, cheeks, forehead – everywhere – stiffness and pressure points at various sites which was getting more and more painful. At one point, I had such pain in my chest that I thought I was having a heart attack. (Much later on, I learned that with severe fibromyalgia, this is a common occurrence, and many others with fibromyalgia had also experienced this.)

It was good to finally be diagnosed with fibromyalgia. At least I knew now what was happening to me physically. In the early '90s, fibromyalgia was not yet fully understood by some in the medical field. As a result, my doctor had put it down to depression, then to severe and prolonged stress, and a few other things. I was given antidepressants to deal with it. I told the doctor that I was not depressed, although I was obviously dealing with an awful lot of bad stress. I had been sharing with her what was happening in the world around me. She just said that this was the way they treat fibromyalgia. Needless to say, I threw the prescription away. The last thing I needed was pills to make me even less able to think properly.

Every doctor I went to asked the same question, "Where is your husband? Why is he not helping you? You should not be driving yourself." When I tried to discuss this with Joe, he told me that he had a stressful job and said, "What is the matter with you that you can't even handle your own mother?" Although I'd tried and tried to make him see just what I was handling, he just denigrated it all and ignored it and me and what was happening to me. He wouldn't go with me to the nursing homes and the Psychiatric Hospitals, so he didn't see my mother in those out-of-control states. Joe wasn't a very insightful person at the best of times, but he should have tuned in to some of the things going on around him.

I went to a psychologist because I needed to understand what was happening to me. She wanted to see Joe. He came with me to an appointment, but he looked so mad. He didn't believe in psychologists. He thought they were all crazy, and he just knew better. When the psychologist saw me, she said, "You look like you've been crying." I had not been crying! Those flashbacks of my childhood were coming into my mind at a terrifying pace, and my head hurt so badly! I could hardly see! At this time, I was in enormous physical pain, and I was having panic attacks. I was barely functioning. When Joe asked her to explain abuse to him, she just responded with a casual, "Well, it's complicated." and didn't explain that statement further. Needless to say, the visit was a total waste of time. The psychologist was no help at all.

Sometimes I wondered if I was going crazy, just like my mother. Yet, somehow I knew I wasn't, and I just kept hanging on. I was just getting through the days like a robot, doing whatever was demanded of me. I was so emotionally traumatized that I just went through the motions and through each day in a kind of daze, flashback after flashback invading my mind. I'd repeatedly asked for help but got none. I had been spending a lot of time with Kayla since her marriage. I was horrified at the situation she was living in, and I couldn't leave her alone in those terrible circumstances. I knew that I was being an ineffective mother, but with the horrific state of health I was in, I just couldn't do more than fight to get through the days myself. When I could no longer verbalize what I had to say, I wrote Kayla a letter telling her what the drinking, drugs, swearing, and emotional abuse were doing to her and to our family. I begged her to open her mind to the terribly dysfunctional family she'd married into.

I intervened as much as I could on Kayla's behalf, and I was seeing some positive results. I was beginning to recognize my daughter again. We spent more and more time together. Kayla and I talked about her life with Grant, and it all began to tumble out of her – how they verbally abused her, criticized her, called her a blonde ditz and the name-calling went on and on (like it had in high school). She felt humiliated. When she and Grant would go anywhere, he would refuse to clean himself up and would go out dirty, reeking of alcohol, and be half-drunk. She told me that she had to do all of the check-writing, pay all the bills, and do all of the bookwork. She'd discovered that he could hardly read or write. She became so ashamed that she'd gotten into this mess with all of those controlling, drunk people all around her telling her what to do, how to do it, and when to do it. Such horrible dysfunction.

The situation was all way too big and way too complicated for Kayla to deal with alone. She'd always been such a gentle, quiet child. She hadn't been brought up in anything like that. I knew she couldn't stay in that dysfunction and survive. And there I was, just trying to get through each day and trying to cling to my sanity in the midst of all this craziness. I was intervening as much

29

as I could for Kayla and seeing all of these great results, so it just blew my mind when his 'good sister' made the comment that "Kayla's making some good changes.", and Grant and his family were taking the credit for those good changes! Unbelievable! It astonishes me how so many things can be so misconstrued.

It is inconceivable that Joe could not see the struggle I was having with my health and did not see what was happening to his daughter. He had to have seen that I'd been losing a lot of weight, looked terribly worn, could hardly walk because of the pain, and started to forget how to do things like making coffee and cook, but he just laughed at me, sometimes appeared mad, and made fun of me – mocked me. For a long time, I couldn't speak. I believe that I was catatonic. How could he be so very blind to what was right in front of him? It was cruel that he could just leave me in that state. It is unbelievable, shocking, inhumane, and unspeakable. It was very severe neglect. He deprived me of the health care I should have been receiving. He neglected his duties as a husband and a father, and I began to think of him as a monster.

****

I had begged for help from so many and in so many ways. My life had turned into a horror story. No one believed that my mother was so hard to deal with. Everybody just ignored what I told them and just left me to it. They didn't want to hear it. I felt totally helpless and totally abandoned by everyone except for my daughter. I wondered if I would just snap one day. I was on my own, not being given any help or support, losing family, my church, my friends, and I was in such a horrible state of health that was getting worse and worse daily. And I was helpless to do anything about any of it. It was all a terrible test of my sanity. I was so very alone in dealing with everything, and my daughter needed so much help and support right now. During this time, my daughter asked so many times, "Why isn't dad doing anything to help?" I had no answer for that.

And how I fought those memories. I did not want to remember anymore. My head felt like it would burst into tiny, little pieces. My life was becoming a blur of flashbacks, ravaging my mind. It was stealing my entire childhood and life away. And, oh God, it hurt – it hurt so very much. And my body was in such terrible, terrible pain. I begged God to stop these memories, but He did not help me – not then.

Chapter 3
Cleaning My House

In 1995/96, I had a doctor's order to stay at home in a quiet environment to rest, giving my very traumatized mind and my painful body a chance to heal from all the shocks I had been receiving. 1997 wasn't much better. Those three years passed by me in a blur and were totally lost to me. Joe had not explained the medical restriction of visitation to my mother-in-law. Darla and I had become wonderful friends over the years. Since my husband had not explained what was happening to me to her, she (and his sister and her family) thought I was deliberately ignoring them. My mother-in-law thought I didn't want to see her or be friends with her anymore. That is not the way it was at all! It was a travesty that Joe hadn't told her about my poor state of health. How utterly cruel that was, for his mother's sake and for mine. Not only did he severely hurt me but he also hurt his mother terribly as well and set us all up for needless and pointless hurt and pain. He didn't tell anybody! And I was in such a horrible state of health I couldn't function well enough to tell anyone at that time. What that did to me will come up a little later and cause yet more damage to me. He told no one and just went on like nothing much was happening. How could he just watch me suffer like that for such a long time? Heartless and way beyond despicable.

****

Immediately after the last drama performance at the church, and while my mother was at the Cedar City Psychiatric Hospital, I began to have this immediate and emphatic need to clean my house. It didn't make sense to me at all, but I just knew that I absolutely had to do it. I had to! Even in the horrid state of health I was in, I began to do just that. I know it sounds crazy, but it just had to be done. Kayla helped, and we had that house so sparkling clean – not an easy job in my condition! I felt so compelled to do this. Something was driving me and there was nothing I could do to stop it. If friends had seen me, I'm sure they would have thought that I was crazy. My poor daughter didn't really understand this desperate need to clean, but she helped me, and she supported me. She hadn't seen me like this before – nobody had! She just knew that something horrible was happening to me. She was doing the job that her father should have been doing. She hung in there for me, and I hung in there for her. (My son had graduated from high school in '95, had gone off to college, and lived in Cedar City, so he didn't see much of what was taking place in our home. At the time, I thought that had been a good thing, but his absence during those years was going to come back to haunt me some years later.)

And then, slowly, it did make sense. It all became abundantly clear. I didn't know what that cleaning was about until weeks later when it became clear that I needed to clean my house alright, but it was the house that encircled my life – the very essence of 'me', my inner self that had been so destroyed by a variety of abuses, mistreatment, degradation, minimalization, and so on – my life that I had to clean up and clean out – clean out all of the dysfunction, the dirt and the grime of all the abuse I'd sustained for a lifetime. I needed to get rid of all the people in my life who were causing all this craziness in my life. This compulsion to clean was coming from somewhere way outside of me, yet deep within me, and was very powerful. And there was this brightness surrounding me now – a light…getting brighter, and brighter. I couldn't understand…

Cleaning my inner house would have to take place a little later on because all I could do right now was just try to somehow get through each day. My body was such a horrific mass of pain, and the flashbacks of my childhood were coming into my mind at a faster pace each day.

I became so afraid of everyone – a terrible fear – panic attacks – couldn't be near anyone. There was so very much hurt surrounding me. I was just a great big ball of hurt. I didn't trust anyone to not hurt me. I trusted no one. I was so afraid that they would hurt me some more, and I couldn't take any more hurt. These memories were ravaging my mind. I didn't know what was happening to me.

****

I learned later on that I had been in the beginning stages of RMR and was now advancing into the emergency stage of RMR – the memories triggered by a church that had initiated that memory recovery and a church that didn't know how to deal with abuse. Oh, I know that there were some other triggers (obviously my mother), but the church was the main instrument in digging out those memories that had been so deeply buried in my subconscious.

****

I thought the pain and this onslaught of memory recovery would never end. My daughter kept saying, "Why isn't dad helping?" The doctors kept asking, "Where is your husband? Why isn't he here? Why isn't he helping you? You shouldn't be alone! You shouldn't be driving in this state." I had no answers for the doctors, and I had no answers for Joe, nor for his lack of action. He should have been home helping his family through all that crisis, but he just ignored everything and started going off on company loan assignments, acting like nothing much was happening at home, and he left me to handle everything. I will readily admit that I could not have been easy to live with at this time. When these memories slammed so mercilessly into my mind, it was terrifying to be living through all of that again. I felt like I was living inside a horror story that just went on and on and on. My life was being ripped apart, piece by piece, and I couldn't do anything to stop it. It was like living inside a horrible nightmare that I couldn't get out of. But Joe and I had been married for almost 30 years. He couldn't help but have seen the changes in me. I couldn't understand how he could just leave me like that. Why wasn't he getting some help for me? I just couldn't understand how he couldn't see that something terrible was happening to me and see the enormous pain I was in. It was absurd and unbelievable. It felt brutal and it seemed almost criminal.

I was exhausted and in so very much pain. I could barely talk or put two sentences together anymore. I tried to help my daughter, but I just didn't have the strength – the energy – and I was going so deeply into shock. I couldn't stand any noise. My daughter had such a soft, gentle voice, but when she spoke, it was like a booming, hammering, resounding banging, and I had to ask her to speak more quietly or to whisper. Those memories kept slamming into my mind. Would there never be an end?

I didn't know how long it had been since I had last eaten anything. I know it had been days, and I had the thought that I should eat something. When I painfully got to the kitchen, I got a frying pan and a steak out, but I didn't know what to do with it. My mind couldn't tell me what to do – it was blank. Some weeks, or months (I don't know which) later, I had to learn how to cook all over again. And I'd forgotten how to make coffee! How could this be? I couldn't read at all anymore. The paper was all a blur of black and white. When I tried to speak, I found that I couldn't speak at all. My God, what was happening to me! I was so scared and so very alone.

Soon, I couldn't get myself into the car anymore. It was so horribly painful to move any part of my body. Therefore, I couldn't get to a doctor anymore. Anyway, the last time I was able to get into a car and get to my doctor, I got lost and couldn't remember how to get there. There was no way I should have been driving in the shape I was in – physically and mentally. One would have thought that a husband should have been taking me to doctor appointments. Not my husband, though. The memories kept slamming into my mind. The pain throughout my head and body got worse and worse. And why was this light getting so bright all around me?

And then came a day when I could no longer walk or move without unbearable, horrific pain. My entire body was just enveloped in such excruciating pain, and these memories were slamming themselves into my mind so hard and so fast now. My head felt like it had been hit over and over and over again with a sledgehammer – a terrible assault on my mind. It was like a band of steel surrounded my head – tightening and tightening. My forehead, my temples, my eyes…it felt like someone was putting immense pressure on my eyes. They hurt so badly. My vision was severely impaired. I was a total mass of pain. I couldn't move, even a little, without intense pain. I couldn't stay oriented anymore. Time was of no consequence anymore. I had lost total awareness of the rest of the outside world. All I knew was the horrible memories that kept slamming mercilessly into my mind. I knew that I couldn't take much more. My mind was putting up a terrible fight to 'stop these memories'!

I lay down on the sofa. I was 100% disabled. If I tried to move, it was excruciatingly painful. I stayed on the sofa in the living room for weeks, a month, two months, longer? I don't know. My life was a constant series of flashbacks and excruciating pain. There was nothing else. I had nothing left in me anymore, and these flashbacks were coming so quickly now – at a relentless, furious pace. I just gave up and let those memories come. There was nothing else I could do.

I knew I couldn't hold on much longer. I had completely lost track of time, days, weeks, and months. All I could do was fight to get through the day, the hour, and the minute and try to hold on, hold on, and hold on to my sanity. One day, I remember getting to the bathroom somehow. The bathroom scale was there, and I stepped on it. It said 90 lbs. My God, I had lost about 20 lbs. My husband couldn't see that? There had been so much crazymaking all around me – a mother who was like a wild woman, a drunken son-in-law who didn't make any sense at all and was taking my daughter down with him, a crazy church with nothing but secrets, and a husband who just was blind to all of it and did nothing. And here I was in the midst of the emergency stage of RMR of childhood abuse. Oh, how hard I fought to live through each day and to hang onto my sanity. Those memories were stealing my childhood and whatever good things there had been in my childhood away. I didn't want to remember anymore! Stop it! Stop it! It seemed as if the whole world around me had gone mad!

How is it possible that I had lived in such abuse? I had always wondered why I couldn't remember much about my childhood. Now I was finding out why. I had completely blocked most of it out. I didn't want to remember those horrible things. Go away! Go away! I wondered if I really was, in fact, losing my mind. Every once in a while, I'd remember that my daughter desperately needed me. Then…more flashbacks. I was helpless to be of any assistance to anyone else because I had to struggle so hard to just hold on, hold on.

During these past few months, there had been brightness surrounding me. That light was growing brighter and brighter. I couldn't understand why it was so bright, day and night. I'd been in such excruciating pain physically and mentally for such a long time. And my head felt like it was going to burst open with the pain of these horrible memories that were stealing my life away. Flashback after flashback was slamming into my mind, one flashback almost on top of the last one. Slam! Slam! Slam! I couldn't do anything more. I just laid there and let it happen.

Those memories were so real. I was living in pure and utter terror – mental torture that the human mind and spirit are not equipped to survive from, and yet I hung in there somehow. I don't know how. I was living my childhood all over again, feeling all the feelings I felt at the time, and there was such a bright light surrounding me – so bright. My mind was just a mad, mad rush of memory recovery. My childhood was being ruthlessly stolen away – the childhood I thought I'd had and the father that I had always loved so much and thought I was so close to – all of that was destroyed. I never could identify with my mother, and as the memories of her ranting, or doing some of the strange things she did at unexpected times, or some of her out-of-control behavior surfaced, it was terrible to have to live through that again, but the day the recognition hit that my father had hurt me so badly during that childhood, it nearly killed me.

I felt like my heart was being viciously ripped out a little piece at a time and then torn out again. That childhood and who I thought I was…all gone in a bunch of flashes of triggered horrible memories of such anger, yelling with spittle running down their chins, screaming, denigrating, being called stupid, hiding under beds or in a closet to try to get away from it all, and the fear, the fear. I was so scared, so terribly scared. Sometimes they could be nice for a little while, then the yelling would start again. All of this was hidden from anyone outside of our family – neighbors, relatives, everyone – so much unpredictability. Nobody knew what was going on in our family.

[*Slam! Suddenly, I found myself at a time when I was sitting on the ground with a rusty, old nail, and I was scraping it harshly across my wrists, trying to make myself bleed so that all of the badness that was inside of me would come out. It didn't hurt physically. I didn't feel anything. I just wanted the badness to go away. I was just a little girl. (I was 7 years old.)*]

[*Slam! They're throwing things and yelling at each other! Their faces are all red! Scary, scary. I have to get out of here! (I was 5 years old.)*]

[*Slam! Suddenly, I was watching my daddy going down the road with his little black suitcase. He was so mad. His face was all red. There'd been so much yelling and roughness. I was so scared, and I hid behind the couch. But my daddy was leaving. He was walking down the road with his suitcase in his right hand, and he said he wasn't coming back. I didn't know how he could just leave me there when he loved me so much, especially knowing how much I love him. How could he just leave me behind? He was leaving me all alone. What was I supposed to do? I probably wouldn't even go to school anymore. And what about in the winter? It would be so cold because Daddy always lit the fires to keep us warm. Mommy wasn't allowed to have any matches. And what about if I got another sore throat? Daddy always looked after me. I don't know if I'll remember what to do. Mommy didn't know how to do very much, and Daddy always had to tell her what to do. Now, I'll have to help Mommy. I was so scared.]*

[But, luckily, Daddy came back. I'm going to try to be a really good girl from now on so that Daddy will never, ever leave me again. (I was 6 years old.)]

[Slam! Oh, they're yelling and yelling. Daddy's so mad. His face is red. Mommy's so mad. Shut it off! Shut it off! It's too scary. I have to be a better girl. Run and hide. Run and hide. (I was 8 years old.)]

[Slam! Mommy threw a chair at daddy. Daddy threw it back. They are throwing things at each other. Yelling! Yelling! Oh, Mommy hit Daddy! Daddy hit her back! I have to hide. I have to hide. I'm so scared. (I was 10 years old.)]

And, those memories kept on, and on, and on – slamming into my mind nonstop. As the memories soared on, I relived my entire childhood almost day by day, week by week, year by year, and it just went on and on as I relived the fear and the pain all over again – back and forth, back and forth through the years. God, oh God.

[Slam! I was 4 years old...]
[Slam! I was 8 years old...]
[Slam! I was 3 years old...]
[Slam! I was 9 years old...]

I was suddenly that little girl again hiding to get away from all the anger, fear, and craziness. That scared little kid was me. I remembered what it was like to be scared stiff. That little girl was so confused. I didn't know who I was anymore. So much upheaval, and so much chaos. I remembered that little child who was so scared, trying to be funny and make Mommy and Daddy laugh instead of fight, I remembered trying to be such a good little girl because I thought I was causing this fighting, I remembered being told so often that I was stupid, and I remembered being slapped in my face because I could never do anything right and had to be yelled at so that maybe I could learn to do it right. With someone like me, there's no other way to make me learn. (I just kept trying to remember to breathe through this horrendous onslaught of memory recovery.) Oh God, please don't make me remember anymore!

****

I had a hard time believing that that little girl was me, yet I knew that it was. It hurt so badly. I felt like, no matter what I did and no matter how hard I tried, I was never good enough and never smart enough. I was convinced that I was stupid just like my mother (I identified with her). I must be stupid. My sister told me that, too. I just gave up and didn't even try anymore because I accepted the fact that I was stupid and could never learn anything. I had no aspirations of becoming anyone educated. That may sound strange because my school marks were actually very good and in the high percentile until I reached high school. That is when they began to suffer. Now I know it was because of all the yelling, screaming, craziness, and being called stupid so many times. I honestly believed that I was stupid. I had spent my childhood trying to make everyone laugh and be nice. I had been a child acting in a parental role [When you are told repeatedly that you are stupid and consistently being yelled at, you believe that you are stupid, just like they said I was. When you are amidst parents who are almost always yelling at each other and you are watching and listening to the yelling and craziness around you, you sometimes blame yourself. That's what I did, and I tried everything I could to try to make things better. When I was young, I believed that all families were like mine. As in all dysfunctional homes, there were some good times, but they didn't outweigh the bad times.]

****

As a child, it made no sense to me that people could yell and scream at each other and then sit down and read the Bible. If there was a kind and loving God, how could He allow these bad things to happen? I had a hard time believing that He cared about me. That kind of upbringing really confused me at an early age, and I never did go to church until my children asked to go because their friends did (No wonder it had taken me so long to trust in the one church I became a member of). I took my children to church, and just look where I wound up! Instead of leaving all that dysfunction behind, I had wound up in yet another place where there was more dysfunction.

****

A few years after this terrible onslaught of memory recovery, I learned that when I was raised in that dysfunctional, raging home, I had become wary, slow to indulge optimism, and I never, ever fully trusted anyone to treat me fairly. I never fully learned how to trust anyone. If you try to get close to someone, how can you ever be sure that you really know them – that they haven't just shown you a part of themselves that they want you to see. Once trust is broken, over and over, it is hardly ever recovered again. My trust was pretty much ruined in childhood. [I've worked on trust for my entire life. The church had seriously betrayed my innocent trust, and Joe had also broken my trust over and over again. I now think that trust is a sacred thing, and it takes me a very long time to place trust in anyone. I'm on-guard all of the time.]

****

I left my childhood home the minute I turned sixteen. For several years, I worked at various jobs. The years passed by, and I 'forgot' my childhood. When I turned twenty-one, a fellow from Manpower approached me and talked me into taking some formal education. At first, I balked because I just knew that I could never learn anything; yet, for whatever reason, he had faith in me, so I relented, went to Cedar City, and took a nursing program. He must have seen something in me that made him think that I had some potential. I worked very hard in the program because I was so sure I would fail and, low and behold, I came out of the program at the top of the class.

For the first time in my life, I realized that I could actually learn. That's pretty sad when you think about it. I was twenty-one years old. I ended up getting the second-highest marks in a class of about sixty students. Being twenty-one and learning for the first time that I could actually learn is a very sad circumstance that most people might never be able to understand. I think only other abuse survivors can fully understand what all that mental trauma can do to a person. I will always be very grateful to the man from Manpower. He changed an important part of my life, and I was able to start believing in myself. It was actually very exciting to know that I could really learn! I wasn't stupid after all! It helped my confidence and self-esteem, but that had been so trampled on, and I have had to work on those two things for my entire life.

Then, when I was twenty-two, I met Joe and made the mistake of marrying him, thinking that I could do no better. Terrible mistake. At that time, however, I honestly didn't think I deserved any better than him. Joe's family were very judgmental people, and it took me about ten years to prove to my in-laws that I was a good person. I never did become good enough for his sister. Until 1995, I hadn't realized that I had spent my entire life trying to prove to myself and to others that I was a good person and that I could 'do things' and do them well. Joe and his family were not healthy additions to my life.

****

There were no rules in my birth home. The only discipline was carried out by yelling at each other. There was very little nurturing in that home. I was on my own, and I grew up all by myself. At the same time, I always worked so hard at trying to please my father and make everybody laugh. My father was the only one in the family that I could kind of identify with, but I was so scared of him. My sister and I never got along. We were too different. In later years, I had often wondered if she was my full sister or not. She had been born much too early in the marriage yet was a full-term baby. She and I didn't look alike at all, and our dispositions were 100% different. She was quite hefty, and I was quite skinny. Nothing about us was similar. I will always wonder. There was something else that I'd thought about, too. My father and I were always together – working together, playing music together, etc. (Yes, believe it or not, there were some nice times!) He didn't spend nearly as much time with Jean. It was like he couldn't identify with her, just as I could not. This was a strange family. Growing up, I thought all homes and families were like this.

When I was about twelve, or thirteen, I tried to tell someone about my parents, and they said, "Well, you shouldn't talk about your parents that way!" I shut up, never said another word about my parents to anyone ever again, and buried all of that pain and hurt – and kept silent until now. Now, how all of the emotional abuse had affected me – the chaos, the humiliation, the putdowns, the degradation, the embarrassment, the false belief that I had a good home, and the very destroyed innocence of the child I was meant to be – was

41

becoming clear. All those years of keeping silent was taking a terrible toll on me. They always said that I was so shy. But it wasn't shyness. I know that now. I was just so scared. It was fear of saying or doing the wrong thing, knowing how stupid I was. Now, I was recognizing how much damage had been done to me in my childhood and how I had been robbed of confidence, self-esteem, and so much more. Secrets! Silence! Don't tell!

The multiple ways my parents, each in his/her own way, caused such permanent damage to me that has affected me for all of my life is of such magnitude that it is hard to grasp words to describe it all. This is when I discovered *the inner child*. Before all of these things happened to me, I would raise my eyebrows in doubt, grin, or even chuckle when I heard anyone speak of *the inner child*. I now know better and know a great deal about that inner child. I have mourned and grieved so hard for my inner child – that child that had been so damaged and died a long time ago – that child that had paid for a lifetime for what had been done to her in her childhood.

In the past, I had done some reading about abuse survivors and had always felt such sorrow for them. Until now, I hadn't realized that I was one of them. I had blocked it out so very completely. As a small child, and even as an older child, I couldn't have dealt with it. I could hardly deal with it now. This was 1995, and I was now recognizing that I was an abused child for the first time. I was 49 years old. My God. My God.

****

I had gone to a minister, a sister and her husband, a variety of relatives, doctors, a psychologist, and a husband – all people who should have helped in some way – and was denied help and understanding. What I told them was so very trivialized, these horrendous things that were happening, including my poor health, were so very minimized, and the truths were so distorted by all of them. These were all people who knew me well and should have believed me and in me, but when the going got really rough, they simply discounted it all. I was suddenly invisible, and they just wrote me off. I have never felt so alone, so insulted, so minimized, so trivialized, so discounted, so wrongfully discredited, and so extremely hurt.

This husband of mine had watched his wife slowly slip into a horrific state of physical health for about eight months now – unable to walk without severe pain, unable to move without severe pain, the pain getting more and more intense as the days passed, eventually barely able to get down the stairs in the garage to get to the car, finally forcing myself to get to the car but unable to get into the car because of the pain, then laying on that sofa for weeks and weeks unable to move at all in excruciating pain (pain I still can't even begin to describe). I had been so traumatized, over and over again, beginning in 1992 while dealing with my parents, my father's death, and my out-of-control mother, causing no end of trouble in three nursing homes and two mental hospitals. I was going deeper and deeper into shock, unable to talk, unable to read, unable to think straight with those flashbacks slamming into my mind, unable to remember how to cook or make coffee, and all this while, trying to intervene for my daughter who also was crying out for help while Joe did – you guessed it – nothing. How could he just pretend that there was nothing wrong? He never once went to see a doctor to seek help or to gain understanding. It takes a monster to watch a wife in that state of health and not 'do something'. It takes a monster to watch his daughter in that horrible situation and not 'do something' to help her. He just did the usual – nothing – went on another loan assignment. How could he just forget about us like that?

****

I had to fight to get through each day. I had blocked these memories so deeply and so effectively within my subconscious, and it sent shockwave after shockwave through me when they were recovered. I was just a little child! So suddenly remembering the bad parts of my childhood nearly tore my heart out. My entire childhood had just been stolen from me. These memories just kept on and on and on, stealing who I thought I was away from me. I just wanted to die. I always knew that my mother wasn't very bright. I hadn't realized, though, how seriously she had harmed me and hurt me by being that mother. It was the hardest thing in the world to acknowledge the fact that the father I had loved so deeply had hurt me so very badly. That part was the worst of all, and it felt like my heart was being savagely ripped out. I was in such excruciating pain physically. It was unbearable. My head – I can't even describe the enormous pain. I couldn't move anymore. It just hurt too much, and I couldn't take any more.

One day – end of March, beginning of April (I don't know. I'd lost track of time a long time ago.) – my husband came home from work, and I painfully sat up on the sofa and asked him to take me to a hospital, or somewhere. I told him that I could no longer exist like this. I wasn't breathing properly anymore, and there was just nothing left in me to fight with anymore. My spirit was gone. I even said that there was going to be another funeral. I was so desperate for his help. He just looked at me, didn't say anything, and went upstairs to bed. I couldn't believe he would just leave me here like this. It was inhumane. I felt totally diminished like I was invisible. I felt totally dismissed, forgotten, like I was a non-person, like I was a throw-away, and like I was of no value whatsoever. It was a shocking reality to understand that I was so completely dispensable, as far as he was concerned. Did he want me to die? Did he think I was pretending? He should have taken me right off to some doctor or hospital, and it would have had to have been by ambulance at that time. It was inconceivable. How could anyone, much less a husband, leave someone in that state of health just lying there in such excruciating pain, 100% disabled, so terribly traumatized, and hardly able to talk? What kind of person could do this? One would have had to have been a blind man not to have been able to have watched me these past months and especially these past weeks and not do something about it.

I just couldn't fight anymore. I had fought a good fight. But I could take no more. It had all been too much for me. Too much had happened to me. There was literally nothing left of me anymore.

I laid back on the sofa. I closed my eyes and said a simple prayer. I merely said, "God, I place myself in Your hands."

Chapter 4
God, I Place Myself in Your Hands

What happened next is so profound and so sacred that, even after all these years, I still can't find adequate words to express how astonishing and miraculous it really was.

I know that I was clearly awake. I know that my heart was beating awkwardly – palpitating – fluctuating. My breathing was so very shallow. I was not breathing normally at all. I know that I was weaker than I ever could have imagined. I was so weak that I couldn't move at all anymore. There was nothing left in me, and I had run out of the energy to fight. I was in such excruciating pain. My spirit to survive was leaving me, and I somehow knew that I was about to die.

Was it seconds later? Minutes? A vision appeared in front of me. At first, it seemed surreal. Although I was so traumatized and so deeply in shock, at this time my mind became so clear and so calm. The entire vision was so very vivid, and I was encircled with the most loving, glowing, bright light I could ever have dreamed of – so very full of such love that I simply can't describe it, even today. I don't think there are words to adequately describe that kind of love. There had been bright light all around me during the past months, which had become much more intense in the past weeks, but this light was, and still is, simply inexplicable. The light was even brighter now, and it was just so filled with unconditional love and caring, and empathy. I felt so warm and so very loved. Never have I felt so loved. This brilliant light should have disturbed my vision, made it hard for me to see (much like looking into bright sunlight), or hurt my eyes, but it didn't. My eyes have always been very sensitive to bright light. The only way I can describe this light was that it was all-encompassing, covering me – surrounding me – in absolute pure love.

To the right, the head of this Man – this most powerful, loving, yet stern 'magnificent presence' – appeared before my eyes. He had very dark (maybe black) hair and piercing eyes that saw right into my very soul. His eyes stared into mine, and the eye contact was like glue. I could not look away. They were startling eyes. During this eye contact, He made it abundantly clear that He was in complete control and had complete authority over all things. He was firm – commanding. In a flash, He put the power and control right back within me where it belonged – all the power and control that had been taken away from me by all of the abuse I had so innocently been exposed to and had internalized. He made it abundantly clear that the power and control that my father and mother (and others) had taken away from me was replaced by the One who really had the power and control, and that was Him.

He was so powerful, and I knew that I was in the presence of God. There was enormous energy surrounding me – us. The Man and I spoke in what I can only describe as telepathy. No words were spoken by Him, nor by me. We communicated mind to mind. To this day, I have no idea how long we spoke in telepathy, but, oh, the knowledge I was given…He was quiet and very still, His amazing eyes penetrating, or seeing into, my soul. I will swear to my dying day that this was the face of God. There was absolutely no doubt in my mind. Even today, I still remember His face. There was such a bright, glowing light surrounding this vision, and it was so full of unconditional love and understanding. I literally tore my eyes away for a time and saw my father on the left side. He was sitting in a chair. My father had had multiple knee replacements, they hadn't worked well, and the doctor eventually had made one of his legs into a permanently straight leg. Now it was bent. He had both hands splayed across his knees, and I saw that the finger that had been amputated years ago had been replaced. He'd had an eye enucleation done many years before and had a prosthetic eye, and I saw that he now had his own eye again. My father looked so young. He looked like he was about 33 years old. He couldn't look at me, and I wished he would, but he didn't or couldn't. I remember feeling disappointed about that. His face was only half turned toward me. It became clear that more than a year after my father's death, he was in a special place. He and Christ had come to me to set all things straight, and my father had also come to thank me for all I'd done for him and on his behalf. He looked like he was being disciplined or being held accountable for his past actions, and it became clear that he was apologizing to me. Although he looked somewhat worried and concerned, he also looked so happy, so relaxed, and had a look of great peace. He was completely whole with no signs of the strokes which had slowly diminished his body. I had never seen him like that before. I felt so happy for him. His entire life had been so very hard. He seemed in total awe as he gazed adoringly at whom I believed then, and still do, was Christ. Was I really looking at my Father and my father? I somehow knew for sure that my father was being well taken care of, and I'd never have to worry about him again. I got the distinct feeling that my dad was calling for me again, just as he had relied on me so much during his life on earth, and that he needed my forgiveness in order for him to go on to that everlasting peace in heaven with God.

Something else – something extremely important and beautiful had just passed between us – been conveyed to me. The feeling of being justified by God came to me. It was like a sanctifying grace was bestowed upon me, and God had found me fully pleasing in his sight. It was astonishing – profound. Had I really pleased God and just been gifted with His grace? Was I justified in God's eyes? Had I just been in purgatory? I had certainly suffered enormously. I had had a very complete life review. I know that I had stopped breathing for some time (I don't know for how long). The next step would have been heaven? But He pulled me back, and I couldn't go there yet. I wonder…In my dictionary under the word 'purgatory', it says "1. (in the RC and Orthodox belief) a place or condition in which souls undergo purification by temporary punishment. 2. A place or condition of suffering." I wondered.

Much later on, I read a book entitled *Justification by Faith Alone* by John MacArthur, R.C. Sproul, Joel Beeke, John Gerstner, and John Armstrong, and it confirmed everything that had been transferred to me by telepathy.

Before this vision occurred, the memories of my entire life had been galloping through my mind at an enormous speed. Now this total life review (which had taken eight or nine months) and the terrible remembering of abuse had ended suddenly. Now there was extensive knowledge being transferred to me but so very quickly, like a whirlwind – faster than that. It was like books of knowledge were opened to me, and the information was passed into my mind feeding me all of the information that I really needed in order to understand my past and all of the abuses surrounding me. I felt like I had one foot in this world and the other foot in another dimension altogether. I was away somewhere, and I'm not exactly sure where, but it was someplace very safe, very secure, and there was so very much love there. And yet, I was right there on the sofa, above myself somehow. It was as though I was in another realm altogether. I know that I was not 'here' for a time.

All of what was coming into my mind was like an in-depth and very thorough counseling session with God Himself. Somewhere I had read that "Our God is the God of the broken-hearted because He Himself endured the heartbreak, abandoned and suffering on Calvary. He promised us the Cross, but He also offered to carry the cross beside us. The road may seem unbearable at times, but every day, one step at a time, we walk closer to Heavenly peace and lasting freedom from the chains of our despair." I think God was carrying the cross beside me at this time.

And then, my special time with Christ was suddenly over, and the complete miracle, wonder, and awe of surviving a near-death experience (NDE) began. He had left me with a tremendous gift of knowledge and understanding.

I was left with the distinct feeling that I was supposed to 'do' something with all I'd experienced and all I'd learned. My computer helped to keep me sane, and I was like a madwoman inputting all of what had happened to me. (I have kept those pages all of these years.) At that time, I couldn't do anything more. Much too much had sped through my mind. I needed to catch up, to digest all of it. I was left with knowing that I had just had an extraordinary and very special time with my God. While all that time (from 1992-1995), no one had believed me or in me, and no one had come to help me, God had intervened and come to be with me personally, giving me back my strength, restoring my spirit and physical health, and giving me the courage to do what needed to be done. This strength and courage didn't come back in a flash. It took some time. I had so very much inner healing to do, and my body and mind needed much time to mend.

I was also left with just knowing that death is not to be feared. After this encounter with Christ, I knew that I would never be afraid of dying. That unconditional love – to experience that was miraculous, and I have never been able to forget it. I did not want to come back here. I wanted to stay in that wonderful place where there was such an abundance of love forever, but He made it clear that I had to come back. I had things to deal with here, and it wasn't my time to die. I wanted so badly to stay there. This loving, glowing light slowly began to fade, and then it was gone. And, oh, how I missed it. I was back here in this world, facing all of the issues all over again. But now, I felt my strength returning, and I'd been given this tremendous gift of much-needed knowledge and understanding. I knew what I had to do, but I was in such a fragile state of health. My mind was so completely saturated with all that had raced through it during these past months. This feeling that I had to 'do' something with all that had happened to me was like a request – like it was my responsibility really – to tell my story and to share what he had taught me in order to help others. It is a very humbling feeling to even suggest that I can be any sort of messenger from God, but all these years later, that request still hovers over me. I can only hope and pray that by telling my story, I will have fulfilled the obligation that I have felt so strongly about for such a long, long time.

****

I had called out to God for help when I had gotten it from nowhere else, and He had come to help me. There can surely not be any more or better proof than this that there is, indeed, a God and an afterlife. I had put myself completely into His hands and had left whatever His will was for me…to let it be done.

****

Because for so many months, my days and nights had been so filled with flashbacks, I hadn't had a full night's sleep in months. Yet, I slept for a good part of this night. I was able to get up the next morning, was in so much less physical pain, and I knew that I had just taken a walk with Our Heavenly Father. I will always believe that I had been in a most holy place with God. I felt revitalized. I felt so cleansed and excited, and my head – my poor head that I had once thought was going to explode with the enormous pain within it and all that was passing so quickly through it – the pain was gone. I have never doubted that I would surely have died if Christ had not intervened and come to rescue me and to teach me so very much. I marveled at the world around me. I marveled at every beautiful sight before my eyes! I marveled at the fact that I was still alive!

****

As the days went by, my body became less and less painful, but my mind had been so traumatized and was so saturated right now. I knew that what had happened to me was about as real as it could get, but I didn't know of anyone else who'd had an experience like this. My two children, I believe, sensed that something amazing had happened to me, especially my daughter. The energy around me was intense, and they had to have felt some of it. But I soon discovered that no one believed me.

The next day, I tried to tell my husband what had happened to me. I'll never forget his words. He said, "Something happened." and that was it. He wouldn't even discuss it. How sad. He could have been a part of sharing what was such an incredibly sacred journey. He had just witnessed a miracle and he'd missed it entirely. This wondrous thing had happened to me, and he didn't believe me. What a pity. Something inexplicable had definitely happened to me. It was an extraordinary experience that rocked me to my spiritual core. There are no adequate words to explain the power and the significance of this special time that I'd had with Christ – and with my biological father, too. I had come so close to death – had died for a time – and no one had even noticed, not even my husband.

I decided to share this amazing experience with my best friend. She and I had always shared everything. She was the one who had told me about the book *When Rabbit Howls*. I'd had this sacred experience, and I was so excited to tell her about it. But…she didn't believe me! That was a shock! I was so let down. I knew that what had happened to me was very profound and that it doesn't happen to everyone, but I was so disappointed when my closest friend didn't believe me. She looked at me as if I was crazy. I knew I wasn't crazy, but when something like this happens to you and no one believes you, you begin to wonder about yourself. Needless to say, I lost my best friend, and I never shared my experience with anyone again…until now.

I began to doubt myself. Was I losing my mind? But I was so sure…Did this really happen to me? Did it? Had this happened to anyone else? I needed some serious validation. Where could I find it?

I was finally able to get into the car without too much pain, and during the next few months, I found myself in places where I just needed to be. For example, I found myself in different bookstores. I didn't know how or why I had wound up there. Yet my hand was reaching for a book that was exactly the one I needed at the time. This happened many, many times. Much later, it became clear how much I had really needed those books for validation. At the time, I was just doing what was put before me. It was like I was led to where I needed to be and led to certain books that seemed placed in front of me. I could never explain how this just seemed to happen. It just did. I think that I was just totally guided by God.

Anyway, I hadn't been able to read for some months, and I was able to read! I literally devoured these books, and they totally validated what had happened to me. I discovered that this had happened to a large number of individuals in various circumstances, and I wasn't losing my mind. I read that paranormal events, such as what I had just experienced, possess an enormous potential for healing. Boy, how I needed that confirmation and affirmation. It took about two weeks of reading (incessantly) many books on NDEs before I began to feel validated enough and secure in knowing that, in fact, I had indeed had an NDE.

A month or two went by. I still needed to validate what had been happening to me before the NDE. I needed to know if this had happened to anyone else. I made an appointment with a counselor in the town nearby. When I began to tell her about the pictures in my mind – the memories of my childhood that had slammed into my mind – she immediately got up, went to get a book, and gave it to me. She said, "It sounds like this is what happened to you." She told me, "You seem to fall through the cracks." She simply told me to use the words "incestuous emotional abuse" whenever the words "sexual abuse" came up in the book. This book is called *The Courage to Heal by Ellen Bass and Laura Davis*, and it helped to save me. I do not believe for one second that it was a coincidence that I'd gone to see this particular counselor. Once again, I believe I was led to her.

I took the book home and began to read it. My God, this is exactly what had happened to me! What the authors had written about – all of it – had been happening to me. It confirmed what I now knew. I really was an abuse survivor! My God. At first, I was so glad that I had found out what was wrong with me. Then, I discovered what an enormous number of things I had to deal with and heal from and what it was going to cost me to heal from all of that abuse while dealing with all the other issues coming at me. How could I possibly survive from all of this?

This book had been written for survivors of sexual abuse, but all the stages – all the stages – applied to me. I began to wonder if I had, in fact, been sexually abused. Why would all of this apply to me if I wasn't?

I was to discover much later on that with incestuous emotional/mental abuse, if it is bad enough, it can cause the same results. The feelings were the same. The healing involved was mostly the same. I know. Believe me I do know this to be true. I had not been sexually abused but had been, and was still being, emotionally and mentally abused. I think everyone should read this book.

For some years, I took this book with me wherever I went, including holidays. I would not let it out of my sight. Someone finally knew and understood what happened to me and how I felt, and the book validated and supported me when there was no one else who did or could. All these years later, this book still sits beside my Bible on my bookshelf. It will remain with me always.

When I recognized all of the damage that had been done to me by all of the incestuous emotional abuse, I began to wonder if I had hurt my two children in some of the ways I had parented them. After all, I'd had extremely poor parental role models. I knew that I hadn't had the tools for being a good mother, and I had relied heavily on parental guidance books and watching other parents in order to help myself be a good parent. I'm sure, like other parents, I had made some terrible mistakes along the way. My God, had I hurt my children? I panicked a bit because I was really concerned. I had read a little about generational abuse and if I had done anything to carry this along, I was going to stop it and stop it now! Once again, this book was magically brought into my life. It is entitled *Toxic Parents* by Dr. Susan Forward. I purchased two of these books, met with each of my children separately and gave each of them one of the books after explaining some of what my childhood and life had been about. I needed to reassure them, educate them, and change things if there were any major problems. Neither child ever came back to me with issues, so I can only hope that I had done alright.

****

As I read the book *Toxic Parents*, I realized that in healing from the church abuse, I needed to reclaim my life from the church just as I needed to reclaim it from my toxic parents. I believe the church I had so proudly been a member of was just another very toxic family. That church seemed to have leaders who were not accountable to me (and to others) in my opinion. Because there was no communication between the hierarchy and the congregation, the secrecy, silence, no-talk rule was in place, festered, and it became just like the family I had moved away from when I was 16. Those at the top didn't meet the needs of the people and respond to us as a family. They just covered it all up – just like any other dysfunctional family. Communication seemed to be from the top down, and we meager congregants were not consulted at all until much later. It was much too late for me! Why can people not just tell it like it is? We should have been handling this as a true family, not in silence. It was very degrading that they thought we didn't have the sense to deal with 'what was happening in our family'. Good families deal with problems together. In this church, the elite hierarchy seemed to have the attitude that they knew it all, and we were just supposed to follow along. I was very offended and shocked at the way they were handling this. We were not a real family. It was a very dysfunctional system. The damage done to me, as a result, was very extensive. I've written more about the church in Chapter 10.

****

I needed to know more about fibromyalgia, too. I was not satisfied with what my doctor tried to tell me. So, I went back to a bookstore and found this book that told me exactly what had caused my fibromyalgia. In the book entitled *The Fibromyalgia Help Book* by Jenny Fransen, R.N. and I Jon Russell, M.D., Ph.D., on page 22, it says that a study had been conducted at the University of Texas in San Antonio. It talks about how, if traumatic events (emotional, sexual, death, etc.) were never discussed with a trusted confidant and the nature of the trauma was never verbalized, an individual could have physical consequences by virtue of internalization. In my case, the incestuous emotional abuse was so traumatic, I had never had anyone I felt I could confide in, and I had internalized the associated emotions via the subconscious mind and buried all of the memories. Those emotions re-emerged in 1995 as the somatic condition recognized as fibromyalgia.

There had been no one in my life whom I could ever turn to and talk about my life – no sister, no husband, no relatives. At this time, with all the horrific issues surrounding me, there was no one who believed me or in me. So, is it any wonder that I was still struggling with this fibromyalgia? I still had to internalize everything! I was still so stunned, couldn't concentrate for long, had been so denigrated, treated by so many as if I didn't know what I was talking about, and the doctor diagnosed this as PTSD. Finally – answers which made total sense.

I still had such a long road ahead of me. My physical health was still not very good. It was to take about five more years before I would become totally free of pain. The fibromyalgia began to end when I dealt, little by little, step by step, with all of that inner pain, all of the immense anger within me, all of the damages done to me, and what had and was still causing it. There was just so much hurt inside of me. The PTSD lasted much longer as I was still being constantly traumatized by my mother, as well as by a husband and his lack of action, not to mention my daughter's situation. My mind was still being so saturated with all of these horrendous issues that had been, and still were, coming at me so quickly. It truly is a miracle that I have survived those *Nightmare Years* in good physical health and 'sane'. Just one of these issues was more than enough for one person to deal with at a time. Dealing with RMR alone and all that entails is atrocious.

****

I still had to deal with my mother and my daughter. My daughter was in such trouble in that marriage. I asked my daughter to read the letter I had previously written to her saying that all the drunkenness, alcohol, swearing, talk of drug-taking was going to destroy her and all of us. I tried to get her to see what her life was going to be like with that husband and his family and friends in her life. Nobody else was intervening, and everybody was pretending that things were OK. Things were not OK, and I continued to intervene. She slowly began to see what was happening around her. I strongly suggested that she should see a therapist, and she did go a few times. She began to talk about leaving Grant. I spent as much time as I could with her, and we talked about her marriage and life with her abusive, alcoholic husband. I asked her if she wanted to live like that for the rest of her life. She deserved better. She deserved to be treated with respect and dignity – things she wasn't getting in her life. I did what I could for my daughter. I tried as hard as I could, but I was carrying such a huge load of emotional pain. I could hardly help myself at that time. It is hard to say who was helping who more – her, me, or me, her. I did get her to see that if she was going to have a decent life, she had to get out of that marriage and away from all that drunkenness and abuse. She was feeling so bad about herself. This was breaking my heart.

Again and again, I asked my husband for help. He just ignored it and told me I didn't know what I was talking about. He seemed totally unable to grasp any part of the enormousness of all the issues I was dealing with. At various times, I had asked him to read a little bit about what was happening. He wouldn't do that, and he just said that he could see what was happening. Believe me he couldn't see any part of what was happening. It was like, no matter what I said, he just couldn't see the whole picture at all. He couldn't even see a blurry vision of the whole picture. I was very alone in all of this. Nobody should have had to walk the walk I did during those *Nightmare Years* alone – nobody.

From 1995 through 1997, my life was such a blur of pain. Way too much had happened to me, and it had all happened far too quickly. I didn't know where to begin to try to get on top of all of this. I had been so shocked so many, many times, and I had not been prepared for any of these things that had confronted me. My husband's lack of action was exceedingly shocking. I was in such a vulnerable state. Looking back on all of this, I really wonder how I managed to get through all of what was going on.

I had had this most special, miraculous, life (and death) affirming time with God, who had given me all of this knowledge; yet, I had been thrust back into this world to deal with so many horrendous issues all at once and in such a poor state of health. I couldn't enjoy my NDE. I really regretted that. I learned, later on, that most individuals who had had NDEs lived a joyous life afterward. But I didn't get that privilege because of all the things that were happening around me and all the things I had to deal with and heal from. I had been given all the knowledge I needed in order to deal with all of the issues, but could I find the strength to deal with all of them? There was just so much hurt and pain surrounding me.

Chapter 5
I Didn't Do This to Myself

I was on a terrible journey. Healing from even one form of abuse is a full-time job – terrifying, terribly hard, and can be deadly – and I was trying to heal from three different kinds of abuse, all coming at me at once. (Yes, I had finally recognized Joe's behavior as spousal abuse.) How was I supposed to deal with all of the twists and turns my life had taken as I continued to heal from all the mental torment? The anguish was unbearable. So much damage. So much to heal from. My daughter needed so much help. Oh, God! Where is that father of hers! My mind was racing, racing, racing. I don't know how I even functioned and got through each day at all. I just couldn't get caught up. Would this ever end! Sometimes I wanted to go to bed and just never wake up. I got mad at God for bringing me back to all of this horribleness – this denial, minimalization, emotional pain, trivialization, and more. I continued to get panic attacks, and I couldn't be around anyone. I couldn't absorb any more hurt, and this, too, was misconstrued like so many other things had been. I had been under such severe, prolonged bad stress continuously for such a long time. I didn't know how I was going to crawl out of this horror story.

I didn't have the time to heal properly from anything. Issues just kept flying at me and hitting me with such a vengeance. Abuse had invaded my entire life, and I had to fight with everything I had in me to overcome all of these horrific obstacles – a vicious, vicious cycle of abuse, opening up scars that ran so deep and leaving them festering and festering. There was abuse in every single corner of my life. Every time I turned around, another type of abuse hit me. I just couldn't get away from it. All of this came at me within a year and a half. How can I survive from all of this? I felt so completely broken, and I was experiencing such gut-wrenching emotional pain. And yet, I remembered that God had come to me to help, so I hung in there. My children needed me. My mother needed me. When I entered into the world of the abused, I just didn't realize how much I was going to lose so quickly. My life was being smashed to bits. And there was so much mourning and grieving involved in dealing with the many losses because of the abuses. I felt like I was on a speeding roller-coaster ride, and no matter what I did, I just couldn't get off.

****

I was originally going to talk about the anguish – the evil – of abuse and what it took for me to deal with all of the abuses I was dealing with at one time. But every time I tried to put it down on paper, I found myself sinking back into the pain, the tragedy, the devastation – the enormousness – of dealing with each one of the issues in front of me and recognizing all of the healing that was ahead of me. I remembered how, at times, all I could do was fight with myself to 'just hang in there, just hang in there'. For a long time, it was like I was paralyzed in pain and fear, and I wondered if I could ever recover from any of this. Even now, as I am writing this, the remembering still has the power to draw me back to all of that darkness. And I have already walked through that twice now – when I had lived it and then when I so suddenly remembered it. I didn't know that there was going to also be a third time in the future. There are always triggers that can dig it up again. But I'll get to that.

I decided, instead, to just say that I sought help and confirmation from a variety of really insightful books, always keeping in mind that all of the books were placed in front of me at very specific times when I needed them the most. They described the painful tunnel one must crawl through in order to get to the other end and in order to become whole once more or, in my case, for the first time. Reading those books in the order they were put before me was like a slow awakening under Christ's protection and guidance, and the jagged pieces of my life all began to fit together like a giant puzzle. The only explanation I can give for the way this had all been happening is that it was like God had counseled me and taught me so much, and now He was providing me with the validation and confirmation I needed and showing me the pathway I must take in order to heal from all of it. Everything that had happened had taken place much too quickly – all within just a few years. It was way too fast. I hadn't had the time to digest and heal from even a portion of what I had to, and there was way too much emotional pain and way too much loss involved. I couldn't catch up. I needed more time.

****

It is hard for me to believe that, even with all the knowledge regarding abuse that is available today, there are still people who say things like, "That's past, forget it," or "What does that have to do with today?" or "Come on, get on with it, and move on." And one of the very worst things to say to an abused individual is, "You're so weak." The person who says that does not have any concept of how very strong and courageous an abused person who is in recovery really is. One individual even made the comment that it was 'good' that this had happened to me! Good? Believe me, there was nothing good about it! It destroyed my entire life, and I have had to build an entirely new life for myself! RMR of abuse steals everything from a person! An abuse survivor has to deal with such enormous pain, and I've come to believe that only another abuse survivor, especially one who's had sudden RMR and had to walk through the horrific and tragic stages of all it speaks of in the book *The Courage to Heal,* can understand. It is very likely that only another survivor can truly understand the depth of terror and pain involved and the desperate requirements and steps that must be taken in order to become that survivor.

One of the hardest things for me to get past was that I wasn't believed, and that impacted me hugely. That my integrity could be attacked like that? That hit to the very core of me. Why would I have done this to myself? Why would I have put myself through all of this? I didn't do this to myself! I couldn't help it that this was happening to me! I couldn't stop it! I tried! It is so very important to be believed, even if the story sounds unbelievable. Having someone believe you and believe in you is a very crucial part of healing. You don't just 'get over it' because you want to. That would be great, but it just doesn't work that way. That would be like saying, "Yes, they caused terrible damage to my life and brought on terrible pain and all kinds of craziness to my life, but that's OK." That is not the way abuse works, and it is definitely not OK! You don't just automatically 'get over it' or 'forget about it' just because you want to or because other people think you should. An abused individual has to spend years (and sometimes a lifetime) healing from all those damages

58

done to them. It does not go away like the common cold does! It is deeply embedded within you, like a horrible disease.

Those things I've mentioned above are the most hurtful words to say to anyone who has been abused. And it really hurts people like me who have been so very strong and so very courageous. I felt very isolated because of the lack of Joe's help, but also because of the disbelief I received from other people (including doctors) when I tried to seek outside help. Nobody should have had to walk through all of these things alone. Yet I hung in there. I don't know how.

A very short list of important things that had been stolen from me and what I had to heal from and change if I was going to become whole is as follows:

1. Trust (the inability to trust anyone/terrible trust issues).
2. Loss of confidence in myself.
3. Loss of self-esteem.
4. Fear of doing so many things that other people did spontaneously because I knew that I would probably do them wrong.
5. Inability to express my feelings because I wasn't allowed to feel what I really felt, so I just internalized those feelings.
6. Fear of individuals in authoritative positions – employees/teachers, etc.
7. Insecurity regarding how to nurture others (the ability to be the loving person I was meant to be and show acceptable affection.)
8. Fear of becoming too close to other people and being very cautious about forming any kind of a lasting friendship.
9. Boundary-setting (hard to say "no" to anyone.)
10. Feeling inadequate, no matter what I did.
11. Ability to be comfortable with myself or within a group.

And this list just goes on and on. I learned that I compensated for some of that damage by being an immaculate housekeeper, meticulous at home or at work, and an overachiever in everything I did in the effort to 'prove' myself. I was very, very hard on myself! Even today, I cannot be in a crowd of people (too close!) because I'm at risk of having a panic attack, sudden appearances disturb me, and I stay far away from controlling people. I still have to sit on the chair at the end of the table, and I shudder (and partly shut down) when I see people angry or frowning. This list is just the tip of a very big iceberg.

I didn't get to be the person I could have been. When I discovered that I could learn, I found that I was actually quite intelligent, and I could/should have had the opportunity to contribute a great deal to others. I was always just so busy trying to survive in a world that I was afraid of – a lifetime of trying to 'prove' myself and always feeling like I was inadequate. There are so many things wrong with that.

****

It must be very hard for many people to grasp the extent of the psychological conflict that goes on in the mind of an abuse victim. I have been told by a counselor that abuse is an entirely different world that many people cannot even begin to identify with. I have certainly found that to be true. I had searched desperately for help. I was treated like I didn't know what I was talking about. What was happening to me was not a reality in the scope of most people's understanding. We abused individuals fight with everything that is in us to just survive, and it hurts – it hurts so very much – to have what had happened to us be taken so very lightly. Memories of abuse do not just magically go away. They must be healed from. We are not responsible for what has been done to us. We are only responsible for how we deal with it. If we want to become whole, we must deal with it. We must deal with it, no matter what anyone else says or thinks. And that is exceedingly hard to do.

****

[Even after all these years (about twenty-five), I feel like I'm writing about somebody else, but that emotionally battered little girl had been me, that ignored wife in that horrible state of health dealing with all of that abuse and tragedy surrounding us had been me, that ignored parishioner had been me, and that wife who was so desperately trying to help her daughter while in that horrible state, without her husband's help, had been me. The memories of those years will always haunt me.]

How was I ever going to be able to climb out of this terrible web of pain and destruction? I was being torn apart. Abuse has such a nasty habit of sending

60

a chain reaction of events that seem impossible to overcome. As well as learning how the incestuous emotional abuse of my childhood had affected me, I was now beginning to see how I was set up in childhood for this horrid pattern of accepting self-blame, minimization, humiliation, undermining, and degradation. I slowly realized that my married life was a continuum of what I had been taught in childhood. I was very young when my father once told me, "You're going to end up just like me." (What little faith he had in me.) I didn't know what he was talking about at that time, but guess what? I did end up just like him – with Joe. Now that I recognized this pattern of abuse, I knew that I had to break away from it if I was going to survive. This type of treatment was no longer acceptable. Before 1995, I thought I'd had such a good life. And now? Now it had all fallen apart. Now I realized how out-of-place everything really was, and had been, in my life.

****

My mother was still in the Psychiatric Hospital, but a new Mental Health Unit (MHU) opened up at a care center in Cedar City. Fortunately for her and for me, she was admitted in the spring of 1996. I was so grateful (and relieved) when they admitted her, as no other nursing home or healthcare facility would accept her as a resident. My mother was still causing a great deal of upheaval, but there was a truly incredible social worker on that floor, an equally terrific care manager, and a great group of caregivers who dealt with her firmly with love and with patience – not an easy job. She was now very heavily medicated and still could cause so much grief. My sister and her husband would go up to see her and, as always, they would upset her with whatever they said to her, and the staff would have to calm her down. I have to give the social worker an awful lot of credit for working miracles with my mother. My mother was still out-of-control and displaying personality and behavior disorders – nothing new there except that when she went to live on the MHU, I wasn't called in to deal with her as I had been since 1992. I only went in to help to reinforce the methods the social worker was using to deal with her to try to get her behaviors to an acceptable level. I readily went in to help her out.

In the summer of '97, I took my mother on an out trip. I did that periodically to give the staff a break and to give my mother a break. She didn't understand why she had to live in a Mental Health Unit. Hmm…On this trip, we talked about her family and she disclosed to me that one of her brothers had sexually abused her from about the age of 10 (maybe younger) through 17 or 18. Oh my God – no more! This was not what I needed to hear right now! I didn't think I could take on any more! And yet I did. I had been on an emotional overload for over five years now. I had been through so much these past years. I was so very, very tired. I didn't think I could stretch myself any further. Every time I saw one issue resolved in my life, another one confronted me. And these were not small issues. It was like a deep, dark hole that I just couldn't climb all the way out of no matter what I did.

My mother's disclosure about her childhood sexual abuse sure did answer some questions and explained some of her behaviors. I believed her. When she had disclosed her abuse to me, she said I was the first one she'd ever told. (Had that been discussed at the Psychiatric Hospitals or the MHU? I don't know.) She had never told anyone. She'd kept it hidden inside of her for her whole life. But she had now told me. It is a great honor to have someone trust you enough to share that kind of secret with you. It is sacred. Because of the damages she'd done to me, it was very hard for me to even see her sometimes. But I had made a death-bed promise to look after her, and I keep my promises. I just couldn't leave her at this time. I had become an abuse survivor only a year and a half ago. I had barely begun to deal with the effects of repressed memory recovery of my own childhood abuse, and I had a tremendous amount of healing to do from that. I was also trying to digest the fact that the only church I'd ever belonged to had brought on that repressed memory recovery by its secrecy and silence, and I was also dealing with all that alcohol and emotional abuse in my daughter's house. My God! I just couldn't get out of this terrible cycle of abuse. As previously mentioned, I had also recognized that my husband's neglect, denigration, denial, and lack of help were also very abusive acts, so I was dealing with spousal abuse as well. How was I going to get through all of this and survive? I got so mad at God. He'd given me this miraculous NDE, then given me more and more problems to resolve. I got angry at Him, yet He was the One who had given me the knowledge, the strength, and the courage to deal with all of these things. Why should I be angry at Him? I was just angry – I had every right to be – and I was so very, very tired of going it alone.

I told the social worker what my mother had disclosed to me about her brother sexually abusing her. Then I phoned one of her siblings and asked some very pointed questions about my mother's childhood, specifically about this brother. She told me that there had been much talk amongst the relatives about this brother being 'indecent' with other female relatives. According to her, my mother had had epileptic-like seizures from about age 2-10. She would suddenly fall on the floor and convulse.

"What was done at that time?"

"Well, in those days, there wasn't much of anything done."

"Was she taken to a doctor?"

"No."

Those were not good answers! I called a cousin and asked her if she knew about anyone else who had been sexually abused by this brother. She said that there had been some talk amongst the relatives that something had gone on with him and some of the family members. My mother was not known for telling things as they really were and could get facts pretty mixed up, but I believed her disclosure. I had just been 'educated' about abuse in this very painful way. And now, knowing what I knew of her life and how she was acting out, I could see that her life showed every indication of past abuse. I didn't need more emotional work, but I couldn't leave her like that, so I supported her as best I could. She was finally getting the help she so badly needed, and I was finally getting the help that I needed and, more importantly, getting some support – at the MHU. It had all been and was such a very heavy load.

My mother's personality and behavior disorders began to make sense to me now. I had just walked through the pages of that amazing book, *The Courage to Heal*. When she had been at her worst – so very out-of-control – I was pretty sure that she had also been walking through all the stages that it speaks of in that book. No wonder she had gotten so out-of-control when she was around men. I think that she and I had taken that horrible walk together, but for various reasons.

My mother was being so well-cared-for on the MHU. The staff was doing such a superb job dealing with her. But…Jean and Ed would go up to see her and upset her. Then my mother's sister wanted to visit her. She and her daughter had visited my mother a few times at the nursing home and had upset my mother terribly. That sister phoned me and said that she'd called the nursing home and been told that my mother had become violent and been moved to the Cedar City Psychiatric Hospital. She had gone to the Psychiatric Hospital and been told that my mother had been moved to the MHU. She wondered, "why." She said that she was going to go to visit with her. Man, oh man, the staff would just get my mother settled down, and then these people would visit her and undo all of their hard work.

Something had to be done. And I had had more than enough. I was in that terrible position of making some decisions for my mother's peace of mind and for her well-being that no daughter should ever have to make. I decided that it would be in her best interests if my mother's family would not visit her. I was wondering if I might have to stop Jean and Ed from visiting too. My mother would be so upset after their visits, and the staff had their hands more than full soothing her at the best of times. I went in at various times to try to make her behave and to calm her. The social worker, the care manager, and I worked as a team, and it was working so well. This might sound a little strange, but the MHU was the best thing that could have happened to me at that time. The social worker, as well as the care manager, helped me more than they could ever know. They just believed me and in me, and that's all I needed in order to carry on at that time. It was such a relief to have someone supporting 'me' for a change. In these past years, I have sometimes chuckled, thinking that it was my mother who lived in the MHU, yet I benefitted as much as she did from the care we both received.

When that sister and her daughter called the Mental Health Unit, they were told that my mother would not be seeing any visitors. Those relatives hadn't been around for many years and certainly hadn't been around these last horrible years. Why do people try to get involved at such times? Of course, I was blamed for being so mean for keeping my mother's family away from her. They didn't seem to realize that every time she saw them, the memories of her childhood and all of the sexual and emotional abuse were triggered. She paid, the staff paid, and I paid. There would be no further visits from them. As a result, I lost all of them. Go figure.

****

While the enormous need to 'clean my house' had seemed a little crazy at the time, it didn't feel crazy at all anymore. I needed to clean out all of the people who didn't belong in my life and were so detrimental to my own well-being – people who were so full of coverups and denial and didn't deal with realities. Jean and Ed were at the top of the list and definitely in that category.

In May of 1997, I wrote a letter of resolution and moved on from them. They had given me no choice. As all of the events had occurred since 1992, they had caused dissension at every turn. I was done. In that letter, I wrote them an overview of what I'd been dealing with, what the cause and effects of their actions (or lack thereof) cost me, and told them I was no longer going to put up with their false blame and criticism when they didn't have a clue what was going on and weren't facing any of the horrendous issues that I had/was dealing with. I concluded with the fact that they owed me some of the biggest apologies of all time. Since I sent that letter, I have never looked back, and I have no regrets for having sent it. I deal in reality, not coverups and secrets. Those things only ever cause pain.

****

The social worker, the care manager, and the nursing staff dealt so well with all of my mother's issues and took the tremendous strain off me. They gave her the best quality of life that she could ever have had. That MHU became like a family to me – a family that I badly needed. They actually supported me, as my husband and sister should have done these past years. They also gave me the gift of time to finally begin to do some inner healing and allow me the time I needed to help my daughter. I will always be extremely grateful for that incredibly insightful social worker, care manager, and all the staff at the Mental Health Unit. I'm not sure what I would have done without them.

I was still not in a very good state of health, but I was gaining every day as I slowly dealt with all of the issues. I learned the hard way that it takes about 10 years to heal from childhood incestuous emotional abuse. The spiritual abuse would probably take a lifetime. The spousal abuse? Such betrayed trust? I hadn't even begun to deal with that yet. There was no room within me to even make a start on that. And what was happening to my daughter was atrocious. Dealing with a mother who had remembered her childhood sexual abuse in the midst of all this was deplorable. I had been through way too much in such a brief time. I'd had no spousal help and no family help whatsoever. In fact, it was the family and the spouse who'd caused so much pain and craziness for me. I had lost my childhood, all my relatives, the family I had married into, and so much more in such a short time. I was so close to being completely broken, but my daughter needed such help. My husband just continued to ignore everything going on around us, treating everything so nonchalantly. I knew I had to hang on somehow. I had two children who needed me, and one was in terrible trouble. I did what I could to help Kayla, but I knew that I wasn't doing enough. How could I when I could barely help myself? And Kayla was watching all of this. She was really angry at her father. It must have been so very hard for her to watch what was happening to me and see her father do nothing about anything. She and I were in such terrible places.

****

Time passed, and I made great strides health-wise. I read book after book – you know which ones! – and I healed and healed and healed. Other than for all the needs of my mother and my daughter, I continued on my journey to become whole.

Summer of 1997 – two years into healing. I still had a long, long way to go. I had an awful lot to heal from – not only all of the abuses but also the loss of families, church, friends, and the list goes on. I had an awful lot of mourning and grieving to do. My physical health was taking a real upward swing. Nevertheless, I was still pretty fragile, especially emotionally.

****

It was the late fall of 1997. Kayla had put off leaving Grant, deciding to wait until things were more settled. Now she told me that she was making plans to leave her horrible marriage – finally! I was so glad! I had dealt with the worst of the repressed memory recovery. There was nothing left buried inside of me anymore! I was no longer in such great pain with fibromyalgia. I was still suffering from PTSD. I can only describe my mind now as being very sluggish. It took me a while to digest more information that came my way. I still couldn't bring up the words that I needed to say. It was like they were there somewhere in my brain, but I just couldn't say them. I was still so very tired – so very worn. I sometimes slept all night and then slept half a day away – all that had happened to me, and around me, had taken a terrible toll on me. I had been through way too much for one individual. My mind was so saturated with all the issues that had been thrust my way. I still had some seriously open and festering wounds to heal from. And I had a very badly scarred soul to try to mend after finding myself in the middle of the spiritual abuse. But I was definitely making progress. Joe? Well, he just came home from work each day and ignored what was happening to his family. I didn't count on him at all anymore.

More 'housecleaning' needed to be done, but I wasn't in good enough shape to do it right now. I needed much more healing time before I could take on any more.

Chapter 6
When Is Enough, Enough?

In December of 1997, my daughter and her husband announced that they were going to have a baby. This was terrible news. It was a terrible shock. It was the last thing I wanted to hear – the last thing I expected to hear. Ordinarily, the news of a first grandchild should have been wonderful news. But not now! And not to them! This was a terrible state of affairs. My God. She had been making plans to leave Grant and begin a new life away from him, his family, and all of that dysfunction. This was not a planned pregnancy. This would not be a good home for any child. I was devastated at this news.

Now, this pregnancy had happened. Leaving a marriage under any circumstances is no easy thing, as many people know. Leaving a marriage under the circumstances Kayla was in – the fear, the control, the confusion, the alcohol, the drugs…With what was happening to me and all around her life, she decided to stay in that marriage until after the baby was born. What a mistake.

****

I had tried so hard to get Joe to help me to intervene, but he'd just ignored my efforts. There is this balance between interfering in someone's marriage and intervening because of what you see happening within it. When you see your daughter living in such a drug and alcohol-infested home and emotional damages being done to her, you intervene! You don't just ignore it! There is a time to intervene, and that time was now! It was past time! But I couldn't do it by myself. I was carrying such an emotional overload, was still so traumatized, and was still not in the best state of health. I felt my health beginning to decline once again. I had already been through way too much, way too fast. I just didn't know how I could take on any more, but for Kayla's sake I knew that I would. Somebody had to. Grant's family was such a controlling family and was extremely difficult and tricky to deal with. My God. If you don't intervene, the worst can happen. And I could see that coming if Kayla didn't escape from that home.

****

I decided to confront my husband about his dismissal of what had been happening surrounding our lives. I was very desperate to get him to help me to intervene for Kayla. I hoped I could get through to him.

One night when Joe came home from work, I told him that we really needed to talk about some things. I told him that Kayla needed our help and went through all the things he'd seen – the drunkenness, Grant's admission of taking drugs, the fact that one couldn't have a sensible conversation with him, Grant beginning to manhandle Kayla, grabbing her by the shirt and pulling her from a room, and so on. Kayla needed help! His reply was the same as before, "Well, she got herself into it. There's nothing I can do." God, what a complete idiot! Did he not care? Could he really not see what was going on? Really? Our little talk escalated. I asked him some pointed questions. Why? When I was laying there on that sofa for so long in such a horrific condition – such excruciating pain (those damn memories slamming into place) – and asking him for help because I didn't think I was going to make it, why didn't he help me? Why did he just look at me, not say anything, and just head up the stairs and go to bed? His response was the same as before, "I don't know." What was the matter with this guy?

****

I had always been a very healthy, vital, and active person. That had changed so very quickly. Joe had seen my health fail very rapidly. He'd watched it all! How could he have just ignored that? I couldn't believe that he would just leave me there like that. And what about his daughter? How in the world could he just ignore his daughter's situation? How could he just dismiss what was so clearly going on right in front of him? It is still so hard for me to believe that he just ignored us and denigrated what was happening. It was astounding. Unbelievable!

I had a tremendous buildup of anger inside of me aimed at this blind, ignorant man. I got mad! I hadn't realized that I had so much pent-up anger inside of me, and I felt like I was about to explode. And that is exactly what I did. I got seething, boiling mad, and I had every right to be mad at Joe! I had so much anger inside of me – the hurt, the harm, the damage, the blindness, all of the negligence…Boy, was I angry! I didn't think I could ever have that much rage within me. He had pushed me way beyond the limit of what any wife should ever have to endure. I've never been so mad, and I never wish to be that mad again. He deserved my anger, but he didn't appear to understand why I was so angry at all. Everything I tried to explain to him just went right past him. He just didn't have a clue! Astounding! He grossly and majorly minimized everything! I consider him to be the most frustrating man on earth!

He just wasn't listening! He just didn't 'get it'! How could he just stand by and watch his family fall apart – his daughter in such a terrible place? Who is this guy that I'd been married to for nearly thirty years? It was just so beyond me to understand why he couldn't see what was happening right in front of him/us. Unbelievable. When I'd been so angry at him during our 'talk', he'd had such a blank look on his face. Is it possible that he truly didn't have the insight to see or understand what was going on around us? He wasn't a very intelligent man, but he couldn't be that blind to all that was going on. Could he?

Needless to say, I got no help with Kayla's situation. I was only two years into healing, and I was still in such a poor state of health. I was so vulnerable. Kayla was so vulnerable. We really could have used some help.

****

With the time I was putting in trying to heal from all the aspects of incestuous emotional abuse and that horrid spiritual abuse while trying to help my daughter, I had no place within me to deal with Joe. Hence, phase three of 'cleaning my house' had to be put on hold. My husband had caused so much frustration and pain for me over the years, especially these last years. It is simply beyond my comprehension to understand why Joe didn't help with any of the issues. As a result, he caused so much more disruption and unforgivable pain. A husband treating all of what happened in his family so nonchalantly, as if nothing had happened, is unfathomable. There was so much he could/should have been helping with. I just couldn't believe that he was just ignoring all of these horrendous things that were happening all around us. This was astounding, ruthless, and ridiculous! He just 'let it all happen'.

When the recognition of abuse had hit me, it had hit me with a vengeance. Joe was such a perfect example of spousal abuse. It takes a long, long time to heal when one has been so very, very traumatized, over and over and over again. I was still being abused, except now I knew it. I just didn't have any leftover strength or energy to do anything about Joe at that time. I knew now that he was not needed in my life and that I would be better off without him. I wanted to heal faster, but I just couldn't. All of that healing takes time, and I just did the best I could.

****

As I looked back at my marriage, I shuddered to think that I had felt so inadequate and had believed that I deserved a husband like that. I could give example after example, beginning soon after our marriage.

In the second year of our marriage, he didn't come home one night. When I asked him the next day where he'd been, he told me it was none of my business. How could I have accepted that? It was a terrible shock and the first of a great many red flags that I wish I had been able to see. When our twin sons died, I went through a terrible mourning and grieving period. He didn't console me in any way. He just called me a sadist. He didn't appear to mourn their loss at all. When our daughter was born very prematurely, he didn't go to visit her when she was in the hospital for the first three months of her life. When I went home from the hospital after each birth, I took a taxi home because 'he was busy at work'. When I was thirty-one, I had cancer surgery. It was a scary time for me, but he didn't show any compassion for me or give me any kind of support. Looking back now, I don't know how I could have tolerated his lack of empathy. When he stole copper wire from the refinery where he worked, I said nothing. When he got drunk, stole a hubcap, and got caught by the police, I went to court for him. I likely saved him from a jail sentence. (He had suddenly decided that he needed to be at meetings in Atlanta…hmm.) Sometime during the early '90s, he had become a silent partner in a vehicle

71

business. When he should have been helping his family, he was always going to the business office. In early 1998, I discovered that he and his partner had borrowed an enormous amount of money from the Deutsche Bank and were not paying it back. (You do not mess with the Deutsche Bank!) I found the letter from the bank in the mail. I ended up dragging him, like a little kid, to a lawyer. The letter stated that they would take legal action if this loan was not paid off and Joe was just ignoring it. I asked the lawyer to explain to this silly man what the consequences would be if he didn't pay off this loan. We could have lost everything that we'd worked all those years for – our nice acreage home and a whole lot more. The lawyer was very brisk and got through to Joe, but it is ridiculous that I should have had to enforce this. Ridiculous. Man, I was stupid back then! Sad, really. Needless to say, the business went bankrupt! Joe's partner did lose his house. Looking back in time, I realized that there had been so very many times in my marriage that I had compensated for him and always, always tried to make all things better – always the little peacemaker, just as I had been in my childhood. I have certainly learned some hard lessons about what a marriage should and should not be all about!

In many ways, dealing with Joe was like having a child to raise. Things were great when times were good, but the minute there was a problem, Joe relied on me to resolve it. He couldn't't/wouldn't look after any problems. He always said he didn't know what to do and left it to me. Now, because I was in such a bad state of health and couldn't look after everything and, therefore, keep everything in order, everything fell apart.

I used to believe in marriage and commitment, so I'd tried very hard to make it all work. Now I had slowly begun to recognize that I'd always been in this marriage by myself and had, in many ways, covered up for him (just as my father and Jean and Ed had done for my mother). Now that I was the one really needing some serious help and he was ignoring it, I realized what a mistake that had been. How ignorant I was back then! And, when is enough, enough!

I have come to understand that Joe was the kind of guy who thought he could get away with anything, and he usually did. I know now that I was an enabler, but I didn't know what that was back then. Looking back, I should have gotten out of that marriage and run like hell to get as far away from him as I could. In the past, I was totally committed to this marriage. I hadn't recognized this as a form of abuse that is insidious. At the time, I didn't realize how this and his complete lack of insight could destroy parts of my life that cannot be recovered. There was going to be more damage done to me at his hand in the near future, but I didn't know that at this time. Right now, I had to concentrate on healing myself and helping my daughter.

****

I thought at least some of the very worst was behind me and that I could now work on healing my mind and body while helping my daughter. All of that mental torture and all of that loss – it just seemed insurmountable. Yet I hung in there. I hung in there with every shred of stamina and resilience I could muster. I just couldn't seem to climb out of all of this darkness and all of this destruction. And too soon, there was more to come.

My daughter gave birth to a little boy in June of 1998. Her situation in her married life was the same. She, her son, and I spent a great deal of time together. She wasn't spending quality time with her husband anymore, as he was always drunk or half-drunk. The situation was bad, to say the least.

In early '99, Kayla again shared with me that she was slowly making plans for getting out of the marriage. I was delighted and so glad that she would soon be out of the horrible place she was in. At last! At last! She was going to leave Grant and take the baby with her. She was very frightened of her husband now and very intimidated by him and his very controlling family. She'd have to pick a time to leave carefully because one never knew what he'd do when he was drunk. He was very unpredictable. She'd recognized all of the abuses within the marriage that would affect her and her son. Kayla was a kind and gentle soul who didn't fit into this controlling family at all. By May, she was quietly getting together things that she would take with her. She apparently had told one of Grant's sisters that she was leaving Grant. It had been a very confusing and very, very tough time for her seeing what was happening to me, her grandpa dying, her grandma doing crazy things, seeing that her father was doing nothing to help with anything, and living in that horrible marriage. My daughter was so worn down. It had all been a shocking, stunning time for her. Me? I just couldn't spread myself any thinner. My health was improving, but I still had such a long, long way to go.

One might ask the question, "Why didn't she come to stay with me?" Her father had pretty much abandoned both of us. She knew and saw how traumatized I was. She saw the emotional pain I was still in. She knew that a very short while ago, I'd had a doctor's order against visitation. She was afraid that if she came to me, Grant would show up and only God knows what would have happened. She was afraid for me as well as for herself. A woman's shelter? Looking back, I should have taken her to a shelter. I blame myself. At the time, my mind just didn't allow me to process everything quickly. I still blame myself. I will always feel like I failed her. It would have been nice to have had a father who cared about what was going on within his family. But we didn't have that. Kayla and I were in it alone.

Chapter 7
Grief Too Great to Bear

On the May long weekend, Kayla was going to make the break when she felt she could make the exit most easily and safely. She and her son would be gone by the end of the weekend.

Well, it didn't happen that way. On a Saturday night, she went to pick up her husband's alcoholic friend. That friend had given her a mixed cocktail with a lot of liquor in it. Two things – in a decent home, a young wife should never have been allowed to pick up her husband's alcoholic friend, and a young wife who was in such a vulnerable place in her life – dealing with helping her mother, dealing with a totally absent (in every way) father, and who was living in this alcohol and drug-infested home and trying to get out of it – should never have been out on the road. Kayla was also suffering from post-partum depression, but Grant would never have recognized that. She died on the road that night – a fatal car accident. Grant's alcoholic friend ended up in the hospital and went into D.T.'s (delirium tremens). While the accident was her fault, it will never be known except by me what a terribly sad state of mind Kayla was in. She didn't get out in time. I was too late. She was too late. She died, leaving that poor little baby (Nine months old) in that drunken, abusive home.

On the night Kayla died, Joe and I were called over to Grant's house, where we were told that she had died. Victim Services was there as well as the police. I'm sure they heard Grant's father saying, "Grant is an unfit father." Grant's mother was going on and on about her six uncles who were alcoholics. Then she said, "I was sure glad when Kayla cut her hair." Crazy. Even after Kayla had died, Grant's mother still had to degrade her. And Grant? Well, he was drunk as usual, kicking the dog, swearing up a storm, and threatening to take drugs. It was all so crazy, and I had just found out that my daughter was dead.

If he'd been any kind of an accountable or responsible person, Grant would never have allowed for his wife to go to pick up his alcoholic friend. He should have picked up his drunken friend himself. That was an awful way to always have to remember the night my child died. Horrible!

I had intervened as much as I could in my terrible state of health. It hadn't been enough. If I'd had help…I don't think I've got it within myself to ever forgive Joe for not helping his daughter. He'd seen all the things I had seen. I would consider it pure, gross negligence on his part for doing nothing. Now we were all seeing the results of that negligence. I will never forget one comment Joe made after Kayla's death. He said, "I always knew she wouldn't have a long life." I still don't know how to respond to that statement.

Me? There had been such a chain reaction of enormous proportions of so much upheaval, crisis, tragedy, and tremendous emotional pain for so long now. Since 1995, I had felt every emotion it was possible to feel, but now…I was empty. I couldn't feel anything. This horrid chain of events continued like metastatic cancer continuing to invade my entire life. It just wouldn't stop. I didn't need any more shocks, but now I had to deal with my daughter's death under these horrific conditions. My mind couldn't take it in for a while. I couldn't cry. I couldn't…I was just empty. It was like there was no place for any more pain or feeling to enter. I was just empty.

My third child had just died. It just didn't seem fair. Sometimes I would just sit and stare out a window, trying to digest all of the horrific twists and turns my life had taken since 1992 (seven years) and trying to deal with Kayla's death. I just did what I had to do in order to survive the day. I could do no more. I was empty. For so long now, it seemed like I'd make great progress in one area and get one huge issue resolved, and then another tough issue would immediately come at me. I just couldn't get ahead of this terrible invasion of tragedies in my life, no matter how hard I tried. And I'd tried so very hard. Kayla's death, under the circumstances, was unthinkable, unbearable, a terrible shock, and I felt grief that seemed just too great to bear. She and her baby had been so close to escaping that horrible place she'd been in. My God. My God.

I had to bury my daughter. I didn't trust Grant or his family to do that because I was sure it would be one big drunken affair. I spoke with Grant's family and offered to look after her funeral arrangements. They said they had never made funeral arrangements before and granted me permission to do so. Anyone who has ever buried their child knows how hard that was for me. I had already buried two other children. Nobody should have to bury three children. After the funeral service, someone told me that Grant and his friends couldn't wait to get out of there and have some drinks. The word I got was that they got drunk, thereby celebrating Kayla's death with a really good drunk. Grant was an alcoholic and went on a drunken escapade after that. No surprise there.

****

My doctor was very concerned about me after Kayla died. She knew about some of the craziness and horribleness in my life, and she knew that I was a very new abuse survivor. I hadn't had the time to deal with or heal from even a small portion of what I had to, and I now had to mourn the death of my daughter. I just couldn't get over the fact – couldn't believe that Kayla and her son (Sean) had been so close to being out of that horribleness. On top of all the other things, I'd just dealt with, I felt like I'd failed my daughter. Oh, I'd tried so hard to help her to recognize all of the abuses around her and tried to help her out of the mess, but I was doing it alone, and I'd had way too much to deal with these past years. I realize now that I just couldn't have done any more than I did, especially with the people who surrounded me.

The doctor was afraid that I would slip back into deeper shock again, and she told me to take six months away from all stress and remain in a quiet environment. That meant staying away as much as possible from Grant and his drunkenness and craziness. For Grant to have expected me to go to his place and feel any sorrow for him after our daughter had died in that way and under all of the circumstances was unthinkable, and I cannot imagine any other caring parent in my position doing it. I wrote a note to Grant stating that my doctor had ordered restricted visitation. My husband, of course, hadn't explained anything to him about my poor state of health, nor about the craziness surrounding my mother being so out-of-control, nor about the destruction at the church. Grant wouldn't have understood anyway. It is extremely difficult to deal adult to adult with someone like Grant because he is so childlike. He didn't understand! Grant was a drunk with the same lack of insight as my husband. Both of them had made such gross miscalculations concerning what was really happening – such twisted logic. Needless to say, he didn't believe me and decided that I was being mean to him. My God in heaven. Will this craziness around me never end! All these crazy people around me – when will it end?

My husband had contacted Jean and Ed about Kayla's death, and they had come to the funeral. Bad idea. Big mistake. Jean and Ed had been out of the picture for about two years now, and that was good. Yet after the funeral, and at this terrible time, Grant and his family were suddenly beginning to visit with them. They were strangers.

Jean and Ed didn't know the past history of Grant and his family. Jean and Ed hadn't seen all the drunkenness and drugs and swearing and sheer craziness surrounding Grant. I believe they only got involved because they were curious. Why do people suddenly show up at a time of crisis or tragedy when they have no business being there at all? Do people just enjoy getting in the way when they have not been previously involved, don't know a thing about what has been going on, and are just there for…what? The actions of Jean and Ed will always be a complete mystery to me.

They didn't know what Kayla had been through in that marriage and that she and Sean were in the process of leaving the marriage. I guess Grant's family made sure he was sober, and his family put on a really good act of a loving, close family when it was anything but that. They didn't seem to see that Sean was so scared of his father. They didn't know that Sean and I were so bonded and that Kayla, Sean, and I had spent so much time together – much more than Sean had spent with Grant. Before Kayla's death, Grant had spent very little time fathering Sean. He had dropped Sean more than once.

Worse yet, and for whatever reason, they decided that Grant and Sean should visit my mother. Grant had never visited her before. Why in the world would he want to visit her now? He didn't know a thing about her mental health. He was certainly not the kind of visitor my mother needed to see right now! Jean and Ed went to visit my mother, and one of the things they told her was that "Grant is such a nice guy." My God. Were all these people just plain crazy?

Good Lord! What the hell is the matter with people who know that she's been in and out of three nursing homes who won't take her back because of her behaviors and her personality disorders, then in and out of two Psychiatric Hospitals, and now lives on a Mental Health Unit, and think that there's nothing wrong with her?

This was all unbelievable. The last thing I needed (and the last thing the MHU needed) was a visit from an alcoholic with no depth of understanding anything about what my mother had been through and who she really was. The last thing my mother needed was a visit from an alcoholic, and if he'd visited her, it would only have been a matter of time before he showed up drunk or, at the very least, reeking of alcohol. It's hard to say how my mother would have handled his visits, but it would not have been good. Grant, Jean, and Ed had not walked the walk I had with my mother – the out-of-control behaviors, the yelling, hurting other residents, dealing with all of the RMR for both of us, etc., etc. All of her behaviors were being so well looked after by the staff. Why couldn't they just let her be! Jean and Ed just didn't seem to 'get it' that Jean's mother was really and truly very, very mentally ill. Neither did Grant, apparently. He'd once made the comment, "I don't see anything wrong with her." Really? They didn't have a clue how hard it had been for me dealing with her since 1992. It's very easy to come in and condemn someone when you haven't had anything as rough as I'd had to deal with.

My mother had a very hard time dealing with Kayla's death. And me? I had just had it with these ridiculous, crazymaking, dysfunctional people. I wrote a letter to the MHU specifying that Grant, as well as Jean and Ed, were not allowed to visit her anymore. This decision was made in the best interests of my mother and for her well-being. It was also done in my best interests. I'd pretty well had it with all of Jean and Ed's denial, pretending, and coverups. And I was sick to death of all the problems they caused. It sure didn't sit well with any of them; however, my mother had been through enough, and I had certainly been through enough.

I'm shaking my head as I'm writing this because I still can't believe how ridiculous their actions were. Did these people all have blinders on? I had written Jean and Ed that letter of resolution and moved on back in 1997. Now I felt like shouting, "Get the hell out of my life!" "Stop causing trouble!" What was my husband doing to help? – oh yeah, nothing.

****

My son went to pick Sean up during the six months I had the doctor's orders to stay away from Grant and his family. After the six months were up, I went to pick up and return Sean to Grant. Sean was so terribly frightened when I told him it was time to go back home. There were times he tried to hide so that he wouldn't have to go. Then he would cling to me and cry, begging me to not take him home, but I knew that I had to. It is heartbreaking for me to recall how scared he was when I took him back to his house after each of our visits. What could I do? It was the law. I wanted to take Sean to social services or to a psychologist so that he could tell them what he'd been telling me. It's what I should have done. It's what I would have done at any other time in my life, but I just wasn't in good enough shape to deal with the backlash that would have resulted. I can only imagine what Grant and his family would have done to me if I had sought outside intervention!

When we would get near his home, Sean would tense up, cry, kept saying that he was so scared, would become extremely tense, had a look of terror on his face, and begged me to not take him there. He began disclosing things to me. He and I had been very close from the day he was born, and he knew he could trust me. Initially, he told me about the yelling, the fighting, and all of the drunkenness. My God, I didn't want to take him back there. This small child had lost his mother, and now they were beginning to try to break the close bond Sean had with me. Why in the hell would they do this – to Sean, but also to me? Kayla and I were the two people he'd been the closest to in his life. Grant and his sister were fighting all the time – so much drinking, fighting, yelling, drugs, etc. I would cry all the way back to my home. Over the years, I can only imagine the trauma Sean has suffered. My husband would see this and did nothing – went off on another loan assignment and left me to it.

Grant and his family knew that Grant was an unfit father (everybody did – it was so easy to see), yet they made sure Sean stayed in that unfit home. Why on earth would they leave this poor baby in his care? Why the hell wasn't Grant's family intervening? Dysfunctional families like Grant's are extremely hard to deal with. Cover it up. Secrecy. Pretend it's all good. My daughter said she had told Grant's sister that she was leaving him and told her the reasons why. The family had to have known that I had been watching all this drunkenness, talk of taking drugs, various abuses, and all the swearing. They had to have seen that I had been intervening for my daughter very heavily and spending so much time with her and her son. They might have seen the letter I had written to my daughter when I couldn't yet string all of what I had to say together in a sentence.

My health was declining again. Seeing what was going on with Sean was tearing me apart. Once more, I fought to regain my health – went on a few caregiving trips and just hung in there and hung in there. I had sustained a tremendous amount of trauma for a very long time now. As hard as it was to go to Grant's house, I did pick Sean up about once a week and took him to my home. We had lovely times together.

At the time, it was beyond me to understand why Grant and his family would want to take a loving, caring grandmother with good morals and a strong value system out of Sean's life, especially when they could plainly see that he loved me back just as fiercely. I was a really good role model for him – so was my son. But that's what they tried to do. They put up every roadblock they could think of to try to make me look bad. They were so unpredictable. I never knew what they were going to try next. It was like it was their life's mission to dispose of me. Why? Because Sean loved me too much? Because he had too much fun at my house? Sean was safe with me, and he trusted me. I think that they just had way too much to hide. I was still very vulnerable at that time. I had been through so much trauma by this time. And there was more to come.

One notable example of their 'mission' came when Sean turned two. It was 2001 now – barely six years into healing for me. In the five years, I had known them, Grant and his family had only ever had drinking parties. Now we were suddenly invited to a 2nd birthday party for Sean. It was to be the strangest 2nd birthday party I could have ever imagined. When we arrived, there was a large group of people there – all adults, except for Sean's older cousins – no one Sean's age, and no one for him to play with. Poor little two-year-old Sean was wandering around the party all by himself. I felt sorry for him, so I went over to him, picked him up, and walked around the yard with him in my arms for about fifteen minutes – in view of everyone. We talked about the trees and the grass and whatever else came up. We had a laugh at certain things. Well, they sure didn't like that! Lo and behold, there was no alcohol around (that I could see), people were all sober, and this was totally out-of-character for them! That was a first!

It was so strange because there would be a small group of people (who knew one another) in one area, then another group of people (who knew one another) in another area, and so on. Groups didn't intermingle. And unbelievably (or maybe not so unbelievably), Jean and Ed were there – the same Jean and Ed who were near strangers to Grant and to everyone else at the party. They also had Joe's mother and sister at the party, and they were also near-total strangers. What was this party really about? What did they think was going to happen? That we were all suddenly going to become one big happy family? Not possible. Sean didn't have a very good time at his birthday party. This party had been about the adults and was not in Sean's best interests at all. It wasn't a children's party. As I sat in my lawn chair watching this unusual and strange gathering of individuals sitting around quietly in their little groups, a lot of things passed through my mind. Were they attempting to make it appear as though they were this wonderful family instead of this very dysfunctional family they really were? If that was the case, it was very deceptive, most people there knew better, and it was a very sad attribute to their characters. Were they hoping that I would get into a fight with Jean and Ed? That would have been in line with, and very indicative of, their crazy reasoning and what they would have wanted. It would show what lengths a family like that would go to in order to undermine or make others look bad. Grant had seen me in a very poor state of health from '95–'97. Was he attempting to use my poor health against me now? If that were true, it would be about as low as anyone could ever go. He would never understand what had really happened to me during the *Nightmare Years*, but he was fully capable of misconstruing the reality. Are any of these things possible? Yes, in a family-like Grant's, it is entirely possible. You just never knew what they were going to do next.

There never was a birthday cake, nor the singing of Happy Birthday to the birthday boy. What in the world was the point of this party? It was silly. It was ludicrous. It was very strange. I don't believe that I was the only one who left this party, shaking my head and wondering what it had been about. In later years, I did have some birthday parties for Sean at my house, but I invited his friends to the party, not mine. We did have cake, we had gifts, and we did sing Happy Birthday to the birthday boy!

Then came the day in 2001 when Grant and his family decided to try to take us out of Sean's life. I had a little red convertible, and Sean and I had too much fun driving in it – they didn't like that. They told me that I couldn't use it when I had Sean with me – strange. Sean looked forward to his visits with me too much – they didn't like that. Sean was too attached to me – they didn't like that. They decided to take us to court to deny us visitation with Sean. Well, that's when I learned that grandparents didn't have many rights and that we were the ones who were put into yet another position I never would have dreamt of being in. We were the ones on trial, not the people who should have been. Our lawyer told us that we must not say anything against the father and be really nice, reasonable people. We must prove ourselves. That was really hard because nothing was said about the abusive household this child lived in, nor of the drinking, etc. The only thing I made sure to mention was that Kayla was planning on leaving Grant. Even though I was barely out of shock, I held my own, and the judge could see nothing wrong with me. Grant and his family did not like that. One of the things they said was that I had pretty much 'taken over with Sean' at the birthday party. Taken over? I had walked around the yard with Sean in my arms for about fifteen minutes. That was it! There were other similar things said, and the judge simply saw through it all. The judge actually complimented me on some of the nice grandmotherly things I was doing with Sean. Grant and his family really didn't like that! We were definitely granted visitation, away from Grant and his family.

Sean was so afraid to go home. I hated taking him back to the mess he was in. It was like a piece of my heart was broken off each time I had to take him back. The fact that, a few months after Kayla's death, Grant had a native woman living with him, she had become pregnant, and he had fathered a baby girl, was kept from me. It was likely one of the reasons they wanted to take us to court the first time. Sean had been told (more like threatened) not to tell me about that. [I learned later on that she hid in a bedroom when I went to pick Sean up.] She and Grant were also fighting all the time.

Sean and I, as well as my son, had terrific visits together. We had such fun. But Grant and his family were not satisfied. I have always wondered if they were a little afraid of me because I knew too much about them, especially about Grant. The truth is that if all those horrid things hadn't happened to me and if I hadn't had all of that healing to do, I would have been asking the courts for custody. But with my recent history, the hell I'd just been through, and with a husband who was absent in every way that counted, I don't think I could have made it through the fight. And with that kind of a family? You could be damn sure it would have been a fight. I certainly wasn't up for one then.

I really can't remember exactly why they wanted to deny us access to Sean the second time, but I know it was something utterly ridiculous. So, we went to court again. It was in 2003. The issues were so similar to the first time we'd gone, and once again the judge threw it all out. These judges have dealt with a lot of families before, and I'm sure they could see quite easily that Grant was an alcoholic and also see that there was absolutely no reason why Sean should be kept out of our lives. The judge granted us twice as much time on this go-around. The judge saw nothing wrong with me, and he also complimented me on some of the things Sean and I were doing together. He felt that it was in Sean's best interests that I stay in Sean's life. Well, that sure didn't sit well with Grant and his family! They weren't getting what they wanted, and I was too reasonable. It's just such a terrible shame that Grant and his family tried to take someone who cared about Sean so much, who Sean loved so much, and who was such a good role model for him out of his life. Really, in the end, it is Sean who was and will be hurt the very most. To try to take us out of Sean's life was a travesty. It is hard to say how much damage has been done to Sean because of all the drinking, drugs, swearing, emotional abuse, sexual activity in his house, and so much other ill-treatment. I'm sure he will have terrible separation issues, trust issues, and on and on.

They always claim that children should be in a home with their biological parents, but when a parent is unfit, yelling at the child continuously, is an alcoholic with little common sense, taking drugs, and so on, one wonders why this is allowed. Families like Grant's do tremendous damage to a child and participate in tremendous coverups. And that is what they did. Everybody around Grant knew that he was a poor parental role model. But they made sure Sean stayed in that home.

In 2005, we went to court for the third time. Here we go again!

A month or two before we went to court again, the native lady who had been living with Grant and had a baby with him contacted me and then came to my home. She and Grant were fighting, she had moved out of the home, and she asked if there was some way we could set Grant up in court so that he would pay child support. Good God, I wanted no part of this. I politely asked her to leave and nicely told her that we should not meet again.

Grant and his lawyer had this native lady in a separate room in the courthouse, but she never did come into the courtroom. I was questioned about her, and I'm pretty sure that the judge could see what Grant and his family were trying to do. It is a mystery as to why they had brought the lady to the courthouse. Did they think that I would lie about meeting with her? Possibly. I don't have a clue about why she was there. Grant had even gone to my husband's family, and only God knows what kind of a story he'd concocted to tell them. He'd asked them if they would stand up for him in court, but they declined. Considering my husband had not told his family anything about the state of my health, nor about the crisis and tragedy surrounding my mother, this all felt very much like a conspiracy against me. Looking back, it is too bad Joe's family hadn't gone to court. If they had, and if I'd shared what had/was happening in our family, I'm afraid Joe wouldn't have looked very good. Grant would have looked just as bad. It's a shame that I didn't get that opportunity to clarify some matters and to vindicate myself. Because I was under oath, I would/could have told them how much it had hurt to be ignored at a time when I needed help and support so badly. One can easily see that my husband's lack of action was at the base of so many of these false accusations that were all being aimed at me – wrongfully and so very inaccurately. Grant and his family tried so hard to find some dirt on me, but they couldn't find any because there simply wasn't any.

This time, they had even brought Jean and Ed along with them to court. I suppose they thought that would intimidate me or make me look terrible in the eyes of the judge. It kind of backfired on them, though. I'm pretty sure this judge had seen setups like this one before. And yes, it definitely was a setup! Of all things, they brought my mother into the picture. Unbelievable! The social worker who had worked so heavily with my mother came to court to address the matter. After what she said, and after what I was later able to tell the judge, you would have thought Jean and Ed would have been extremely embarrassed and left for home with their tails tucked between their legs. They should have been very ashamed of themselves! I had asked Jean to become an alternate guardian for our mother, and she had declined. I don't think the judge viewed that in positive terms. Then, the fact that Jean and Ed hadn't known Grant or any of his family until after Kayla's death came up. They had been invited to Grant and Kayla's wedding but had not gone to it. Then the fact that my mother did not want to see them because they did nothing but upset her came up. Maybe the judge was asking himself the same question I was asking myself. What did my mother have to do with the kind of grandmother I was? And that was the real issue here. There were a few other petty and ridiculous things that came up too. Once again, the judge commended me on some of the things I was doing with Sean. There was nothing wrong with us – specifically, with me. As a matter of fact, I believe the judge could see deeper into what was really going on, granted us even more time with Sean, and that really made Grant and his family mad.

Three times now, the judges had thrown out all of the crazy things Grant and his family had tried to accuse me of. Sean and I were very close. He was a very frightened little boy and was in a terrible situation. He really needed me in his life. Could Grant and his family really not see this? Nevertheless, it was really hard not to walk away from this. It was very unfair that I was accused of things that I was not capable of doing. I only ever had Sean's best interests at heart, and the judges had seen that.

Grant's lawyer came to speak to Joe, our lawyer, and me very soon after court was over. He looked somewhat frazzled and said that he couldn't believe the reaction of Grant, his family, and Jean and Ed. I guess they were infuriated. And Grant was likely having one of his childish tantrums. The lawyer said he had to get away from them for a while. I believe that was when Grant's lawyer realized what a crazy, dysfunctional family he'd taken on as clients. His sympathy appeared to be with me. I heard that, not long after this time, this lawyer switched from family law to corporate law. No wonder.

I sincerely hope that, today, laws have changed regarding grandparents' rights. I hope grandparents are allowed to speak their truths more freely and are taken more seriously. It is the children who pay the price, as in Sean's case.

Grant and his family were very much a big part of those *Nightmare Years*. Grant and his family had made very deliberate and very vicious attacks on my life – all baseless, pointless, needless, and so out of line and nonsensical that it was ridiculous – not to mention a real waste of money. They weren't concerned about my husband at all. Joe was no threat to them. He hadn't helped me to intervene for our daughter. He'd just watched it all happen and done nothing – didn't see the big picture at all. So they didn't attack him like they attacked me. I should mention too how hard it was to get people to stand up for me in court. Even though they knew how bad the situation was and how unfit Grant is as a father, there was no one who knew Grant and his family who wanted to cross them and tell the truths about them. They were just too afraid of what the family would do to them. The words of Grant's partner will always ring in my ears, "Boy, are you people in for it." And boy, was he ever right!

These three court cases were very humiliating and took a lot out of me. Grant's family was ruthless, and it was so very undeserved. There is something so very unjust about the fact that I felt I had to exonerate myself when I hadn't done anything wrong. I am so tired of being everybody's scapegoat. Honestly,

I don't know how, after all that I'd been through since 1992, I was still hanging in there.

****

Joe had never liked Grant and could barely tolerate him. Yet now, it was like he was playing some kind of a victim and letting me take the fall for all of his lack of action – setting me up to be discredited and humiliated. During these court cases, it almost seemed like he sided with Grant, which was rather shocking and totally ridiculous. There had been so many red flags concerning Grant, and Joe had simply ignored all of them. He'd done absolutely nothing to help me when I was in that horrible state of health and trying so hard, even then, to try to save our daughter and get her out of that abusive alcohol and drug-infested house. He had seen what was going on in our daughter's home and done nothing. He just proved, once again, how he treats most things with such indifference and rejects most realities unless someone aims some accusations against him or tries to hold him accountable for his actions (or lack thereof, as in his case). A guy like him causes an awful lot of damage. I know. He's certainly done a number on me. I've paid very heavily for Joe's lack of action. The house-cleaning that I needed to do (concerning Joe) was coming much closer now, but I needed more healing time.

Grant and his family finally gave up trying to find a reason for taking me out of Sean's life. That was a good thing! From 2005 to 2013, I went to pick Sean up and return him to that home, as hard as it was for me. Sean kept disclosing many things to me. (It came as no surprise at all when he told me that Jean and Ed were not visiting with them anymore.) I knew that if I said or did anything to upset Grant, we would wind up back in court, so I kept quiet. My son got married in 2007. My son and daughter-in-law eventually had two children, and when I picked Sean up for our visits, we would all get together. We had so many good times. Sean started talking about a different native woman staying at his house and saying that his dad would be happy tomorrow because she was spending the night with him. He spoke about his aunt (the anorexic) who wouldn't eat anything for 2–3 days, then eat a meal, and proceed to throw it all up, he spoke of a friend of Grant's who was having sexual intercourse with Sean's female dog (That is called bestiality!), and he spoke of a lot of other similar things. I could hardly bear it, and I just tried my best to be as good a role model to Sean as I could. I had lost much respect for the entire system – the way good grandparents were so bound and tied and the dysfunctional families of these children were protected. You know – "children should always go back to their biological families," no matter what further damages will be done to them. Good grandparents are at a stalemate and end up like me, watching this child in that abusive, drunken home with so much craziness – sex with a dog, native women sleeping over to make dad feel good, afraid to go home, constant yelling, chaos, and craziness, etc., etc. – and not able to do anything about it.

****

These visits with Sean worked really well until he was 14, and he was caught performing oral sex on my other grandchild at my house. He had, apparently, done this on his previous visit as well. My God, my God. I'd be willing to bet that this had been done to Sean and maybe much worse. The police agreed with this assessment. It was at this time that the police went to Sean's school, spoke with Grant, and only God knows what happened to Sean when they got home. Grant apparently decided to quit drinking STAT and went into the hospital in DT's. This happened in 2013. Sean was 14 years old, and the grandchild that he had molested was only four years old. Because I know a great deal about repressed memory recovery now, I will always worry that this will come back to haunt my young grandchild in the future when/if he is in some sort of crisis.

And here, again, is another perfect example of a child being left in a totally dysfunctional home where it was wide open for worse and further abuse for Sean, with the pathway for Sean to learn how to do all the things his father did and with a family surrounding him who can do a tremendous coverup. I am so tired of coverups. I know that if you don't take a child out of a bad home when they are young, they think that is the way it always is in all homes. I know that because I was that child once, a long time ago. Poor Sean. I'd had more than I could take of Grant and his toxic family. I never wanted to see any of them again. They'd caused me nothing but pain. Unfortunately, at that time, I just couldn't hang in there for Sean anymore. I needed to support my young grandchild (who had been molested) and my son and daughter-in-law.

So, you know what I did – still more 'house-cleaning.' I felt deep regret and deep sadness leaving Sean in that terrible home, but as a grandparent I had so few rights, and I had been through enough at Grant's hand. I could/would take no more. I will never understand how Grant's family could leave Sean in that home. I can only pray for Sean and hope that one day, he will see the broader picture of what his life really entailed. I pray that one day, he will recognize the abusive situation he's lived in and find the strength and courage to crawl out of it, just as I had to do. Not at all easy. I do know that Sean is totally controlled by his father – the power figure. And, as many individuals know, it is not easy to live with an alcoholic. At that time, I had to step away from the situation. I'd been on an emotional overload for way too long. I'd had more than enough. I needed some peace and joy in my life.

****

I didn't see Sean again until 2018. He was working in a store that I went into. I didn't recognize him until he came up to me and identified himself. He had earrings, a partial beard was very thin, and didn't look very happy. He hadn't grown very tall. We spoke, but it was a strange conversation. First of all, he said he was upset with me because I hadn't wished him a happy birthday when he'd turned eighteen. That was strange, under the circumstances. Then he proceeded to say how he and his father were still living together and still dealing with the death of his mother. How sad for Sean. His mother had died in 1999 (nineteen years ago), and one can only wonder what this child has been told, how he has been damaged, and what he has been led to believe. He was twenty now, and it was sad for me to see that he was getting no further education and that he was not at all well-spoken. I wondered if he was also drinking, taking drugs, and involved in sexual acts that were inappropriate. He just didn't look healthy. I remembered how traumatized he was as a small child, and I wondered how much more damage had been done to Sean. My heart will always just ache for him. Sean will likely never know that he could have had such a good life. This could have/should have ended so differently.

After seeing Sean again, I went home feeling so very sad – sad for him, of course, but sad for me that I hadn't had the stamina to keep fighting for him and for his well-being. But when does that time come when you've just had too much to handle? I'd dealt with so much dysfunction for so long – for my whole life really. I had suffered so very much because of all the dysfunction, denial, etc.

After Sean had molested my other grandson, I didn't think I could ever have a relationship with him again. But now that I'd seen him again, knowing what his early childhood had been like, and likely, what he was still living in, made my heart ache so badly for him. In all good conscience, could I just walk away from him again? Now, seeing Sean so sad-looking and beaten-down made me wonder if I could do something to help him at this late date. Seeing Sean again reignited my desire to help him if I could or if he'd let me. Was I now in a position to try to get Sean to understand that there's a life out there that is so much better than the life he is living? Was I strong enough to get myself reinvolved with Sean? I'm seventy-six years old!

I decided to start sending him birthday cards and Christmas cards. In each card, I write a little about who his mother was and what she would have wanted for him. I remind him of the good times we'd shared before he'd turned fourteen. Maybe something I say will stroke his mind and get him to recognize that there is a better way to live. There is no way I want to be anywhere near Grant ever again, but maybe in time and with a little constructive support, Sean will eventually find a way to rise above his childhood and see that better way. If he does, I want him to know that I will be here to help him. Maybe God will guide me and show me what to do, as He has done so many times before.

Chapter 8
Wasted Years

From about 2000 to 2004 (when Joe retired from his job and began to go on loan assignments more often), I did a lot of reading about people like Joe and really studied his behaviors. Just like the books that were placed into my hands at just the right time regarding spiritual abuse and incestuous emotional abuse, there were books out there that were again placed into my hands – books that described my husband perfectly (the emotional abuser), and they also described me perfectly (the emotionally abused wife).

First and foremost, I learned that Joe would never be accountable for his lack of insight, nor for his doing nothing to help his wife and daughter. He doesn't have the insight for it. He didn't have the insight for dealing with any of the things I had dealt with during the *Nightmare Years*. Many times, I had tried to explain to him what was happening, but he just discounted it and guffawed it. He didn't even try to understand. He always knew better. I was so traumatized, so I'd asked him to read parts of books that explained what was happening, but he wouldn't do that. He claimed that he could see what was going on. Nonsense! He totally diminished everything I tried to tell him. His insults, accusations, denigration, and criticism were so very unjustified. Heartless. He just seemed to be immune to others' pain – my pain.

I went from reading books on healing from spiritual abuse to *The Courage to Heal* to books about spousal abuse, and I discovered that the basic healing pattern is very similar. I just kept hanging in there as I read about the various types of abuse and the damages done to an individual by each type. I learned that none of this had been my fault. These were all things that had been done to me, and here I was, having to deal with all the pain people had caused for me. I had done nothing wrong. I had found myself in the middle of dealing with multiple really tough issues within a very short time, and I had wound up in a terrible state of health. Did I ask for all of these things to happen to me so quickly? No! I would be the first person to say that I am not perfect, but nobody deserves to be treated the way I'd been treated.

****

When I had recognized my childhood incestuous emotional abuse, I had also slowly begun to recognize that I had been in a continued pattern of abuse in my marriage. I knew that I had married a man of limited intelligence (much like my father had done), and I had also mothered him, just like I had mothered both of my parents. I had learned early on that Joe could barely read or write. He had barely been able to make 50% in school and had barely passed his grades. When I had asked him to read part of the book *The Courage to Heal*, he just looked at it and told me, "This book is too big, and it would take me too long to read it." I'd only asked him to read the section on trust, but he wouldn't do it.

I slowly began to recognize that I'd spent all of our married years covering up for him, making him look much better than he was. I'd been an enabler! And boy, was I paying for that now! Back then I didn't know that there was a better way. I sometimes can't believe how ignorant I was. I began to see that as a severely emotionally abused child, I had re-enacted that abuse by marrying an emotionally abusive husband. I have learned that this is a very destructive pattern that absolutely must be broken and changed in order for one to have a comfortable emotional life. Joe seemed to have the need to criticize me, condemn me, and look down on me because he felt his needs were more important than mine. I was never good enough for him or for his family. Now, when I needed help so badly, he just ignored my needs and gave me no support whatsoever. It was so easy to blame me for everything that was going wrong, and he couldn't see that by not doing anything to help, he was adding so much anguish and disorder to my life. He was misconstruing so many, many things, thereby making everything so much harder for me. And by not telling anyone what had happened, he had made 'me' look bad. For example, he had told people what 'he' thought they should hear instead of what the reality really was. At one point, he'd even said, "Don't talk to anyone unless I'm there." How dare he! I wasn't allowed to feel what 'I' felt. What I felt was unimportant and always devalued. And I wasn't allowed to tell my truths. Now I realize that he just didn't have the depth of understanding for any part of what was happening to me or to his daughter. Believe me, I will never allow Joe's (or anyone's) limited perception to define me ever again!

People like Joe have no concern for anyone else and only think about themselves. People like him are morally reprehensible, don't appear to have a conscience, and show no remorse. I learned that Joe has what they call a God Complex – an unshakable belief that he is smarter, and actually superior, in what he thinks he is seeing, is near-perfect, and can get away with almost anything – a guy who thinks he is infallible and has zero empathy or insight. He really thinks he is always right and can never do any wrong, so it's got to be the other guy who's done wrong. He speaks of his personal opinions as though they were unquestionably correct, no matter how wrong they really are. He is very dogmatic in his views and cannot, or will not, open up his mind to the reality of the situation. People like Joe don't know how to respond to people like my daughter and me who were crying out for help. People like him don't see how their lack of action affects others in negative, destructive ways. His neglect of husbandly and fatherly care and responsibility was unbelievable and totally reprehensible. He is possibly narcissistic in that he felt entitled, was quite pompous and arrogant about what he thought he was seeing, and was most concerned about making more and more money – was consumed with it. I had been dealing with multiple issues that were way beyond his comprehension. As a result, he didn't deal with any of it. He just did the usual – nothing – and allowed me to take all the flack. And he felt justified like he was some kind of a hero! He always said that he could see what was happening to me and around us. That was so far off the mark. He had absolutely no idea. He simply didn't/couldn't see the big picture at all.

I have uncovered and dealt with all of the repressed anger I have felt toward Joe. I really let him have it a few times, and he certainly deserved those angry words. It felt really good to show him all of my anger, it had been a long time in coming, and I'm sure it helped me to heal from all the things he'd done to me. But it was like he didn't know what I was angry about. It went right over his head.

****

Over the years, I have tried very hard to forgive Joe, but if I can't truly forgive from my heart, it is not true forgiveness, is it? Somewhere, I had read, "I will forgive him if I can and forgive myself if I can't." At that time, I forgave myself. Looking back over my marriage, I realized that I had outgrown him very soon after we were married. I feel like, except for my children, the years I had put up with him were wasted ones. I'd made a terrible mistake in marrying him and an even bigger mistake in thinking that I had to remain in that marriage.

****

I began to be very glad when Joe went off on those loan assignments. It gave me a chance to heal my mind and body. My mind rested when he was gone. It was like I could breathe more easily when he wasn't around me. Not only did it allow me the time I needed to mourn and grieve for Kayla's death, but it also allowed me time to heal from my childhood abuse and from the spiritual abuse. It gave me a chance to finally see Joe for who he really was (is). I was glad he was gone, and I got very agitated when he came home approximately once a month. All of that minimalization, trivialization, misconstruing of facts, diminishing me, and the total abandonment of me and of our daughter when we'd needed him the most – how had I never realized how being married to a guy like Joe had been so damaging to me (us)? I finally realized that I hadn't deserved any of that – finally! I also finally realized that it was totally futile for me to try to explain what was happening to Joe and a waste of my energy – energy that I badly needed to preserve in order to survive. When God had given me the gift of understanding, He had flooded my mind with all of that knowledge about abuse and what it can do to an individual. Before my repressed memory recovery and the NDE, I was the one who was blind. My eyes were now wide open! I'd received some pretty intense counseling!

****

Each month, my husband would come home from the loan assignments he went on and would stay for either a weekend or for a week. He sent flowers for my birthday and other holidays – did things a regular husband would do,

94

and acted like 'nothing had happened' and 'everything was just fine'. As for me, I just healed and healed and was well on my way to becoming whole. Joe came home for Christmas, 2007. He was home for about a week then, on December 26, he left to go on a loan assignment in the United States.

That day, I got a strange phone call at about 4 p.m. from a female who lived in the Maritimes. She told me that she was the caretaker at the building where Joe was going to rent an apartment in the States. She proceeded to say that there had been a flood in the apartment, and I was to notify him. Then, out of the blue, she said, "By the way, I'm his girlfriend." Just what I needed – another shock. I hadn't had enough of those? (Merry Christmas!) She went on to say that he'd been sleeping with her and had been sleeping with another woman down East for the past years, but now she was his girlfriend. She even gave me the other female's name. I hung up, phoned Joe, told him what I'd just heard, and asked him if it was true. I think I caught him off guard, and he simply said, "Yes." I called him a bastard and hung up. Just like that, my marriage was over. He'd always known I would never accept an adulterer for a husband. Why would he think he could just keep me dangling here at home while he went off screwing his way through Eastern Canada and the Maritimes? After all the other things he'd done to me – misconstruing everything to make me look bad, withholding truths, the minimalization, and trivialization – all of it – all the damages he had done to me – it was going to end now. I had bided my time, and I'd hoped to have more time to heal, but that was impossible now.

****

After that strange phone call on 26 Dec/07, I took one month off – the month of January – to digest some of this, to come to grips with all of the things my husband had done (and not done), and to digest his newest misdemeanors and all of the adultery. On New Year's Eve, I phoned the mistress down East. She enlightened me about a great many things. She told me that she had been sleeping with him for some years and had wondered why he kept on going 'home'. He had told her that he wasn't married. Nothing like being invisible! I had just discovered that he had what amounted to a common-law wife. In my eyes, if not legally, that seemed akin to bigamy. And, let's face it, it isn't just every woman who gets to be the legal wife and 'the other woman' at the same time! She told me that it was the week of my son's wedding that she found out he was married and that he was now sleeping with a female that she employed in the Maritimes (the one who had called me). In a crude kind of way, she shared that "they had been going at it like a pair of rabbits." She kicked him out of her house. She didn't want to have anything to do with him anymore. Well, neither did I! My God, the two females knew each other! The word sleazy comes to mind! I guess that's why he had come to our son's wedding looking so upset and was so different. He would hardly even look at me and wasn't communicative at all. From further phone calls from other women, I learned that there were other women involved with him as well. The very idea of what he had been up to while on those loan assignments the past few years was actually very sickening, and it showed, even more, his complete selfishness and lack of morals. My God, while I was back there trying to regain my health and dealing with all these horrific issues, he'd been having a good old time with the boys – and with the girls too!

Anyway, I should have guessed that he was doing things a married man shouldn't be doing. When he came home one time, and I noticed that he had shaved his bushy eyebrows, he blushed like a little girl when I commented on it. When he'd been working on his laptop one time, I came into the room, and he so suddenly (and suspiciously) turned the laptop off and closed it. I suspected he was up to something that I wasn't supposed to know about. He thought he had such big secrets that he was hiding from me. (Actually, he did.) Little did he know that I didn't really care anymore. I don't think that he will ever realize that, as far as I was concerned, our marriage had ended the day he'd left me laying on the sofa in that horrible state of health. All the damages he'd done to me? What little respect I had left for him simply disappeared. I had trusted him so blindly for so long. Now that complete trust that I'd so naively given to him was long gone.

****

It was a long time in coming, but it was way past time to do that 'house-cleaning'. I just couldn't allow him to damage me anymore. He'd stepped way beyond all boundaries. I had put up with way more than any wife should ever have to. I had gone far above and beyond what should be expected from a wife, and I had done nothing but suffer in return.

In the strangest sort of way, Joe had done me a favor. In January 2008, I filed for an immediate separation, based on the grounds of adultery. I wanted a divorce from him ASAP. In the past, I had never believed in divorce for so many, many reasons. It causes such division within families, and it is especially hard on the children, no matter what their age is. But this man was more than an adulterer. He had denied medical treatment for me, he had left his daughter in a horribly abusive marriage without doing anything, and he had left me in so very much physical and emotional pain dealing with horrendous crises and tragedies. I believe that he had left me on that sofa to die. I believe that if he had helped me to intervene for our daughter, she might be alive today. Placing blame is never a good thing. I'll leave it up to the reader to think what you will about Joe's lack of action concerning his daughter. I never wanted to see him, or hear from him, ever again. I was not going to let him ruin another day, hour, or moment of my life! During the month of January, I stayed at home and made a visit to the doctor to have myself tested for STDs. This man was a serial adulterer, and who knows what he may have brought home.

In early January, I got the first of a number of e-mails from Joe. "I'm so very sorry. I know I did wrong. Now I probably have lost you, and I've lost ..." I actually laughed aloud when I read the first e-mail. It is interesting to note here that he wouldn't/didn't sign the separation agreement until late October/08. I'll never know why.

He wasn't worth spending much time on, but during this month, I mourned and grieved the 38 years I had wasted on him. I went over the chain reaction of all the things that had happened because of his lack of action, thereby placing me in the position of dealing with all of that crisis, etc., alone. It also put me in the position of taking all the flack. Oh, he accused me of being controlling (and a lot of other things), but there is a huge difference between being controlling and taking control. From 1992 on, I took control of all of the situations. I took control because nobody else was, and somebody had to.

I called Joe everything from a sleaze-bucket to a jerk-ass to a slimebag to a f... well, let's just say I made up some words that I wish I could remember because they were really appropriate and very descriptive of an abusive, adulterous man who didn't take care of his family. In my opinion, he was a sleaze-ball who was a danger to me. Let one of his mistresses put up with what he dishes out! Men like him are very shallow and selfish, only concerned about their own gratification and only consider their own needs.

He had been deceiving me for a very long time. I realized that he wasn't at all worthy of someone like me with good moral standing and a person of real value. I had stood behind him for so long and covered for all of his indiscretions (and there were many). I realized that all those years, I had made things nice for him, helped him to 'grow up' (as his mother had once told me), and this is how he was thanking me. What a complete waste of my time – thirty-eight years. His actions (especially since 1995) were just plain appalling and beyond cruel. He had just treated everything that had happened like it was a terrible inconvenience for him and like he was the one long-suffering and 'oh, so noble' when he had done nothing to help. And the promise he had made "for better or for worse, in sickness and in health" was completely broken and forgotten by him. Really, he was such a coward for not facing up to things that were happening all around us. I should have kicked him out of my life so much sooner. What a fool I had been for thinking that I had deserved someone like him for a husband.

All of these things were going back and forth in my mind, and I just kept shaking my head. What more could he do to me? If he thought he could break me, I was simply not going to let that happen – not after all I'd been through. I felt no sorrow at his exit from my life. And if he ever thought that I was back here weeping and bawling and carrying on…well that would be giving himself way too much credit because there was no place in my life for a guy like him. I felt nothing but relief.

Then, toward the end of January, I realized that I would never have to deal with him ever again, and the mourning and grieving ended on a very happy note. I would never have to deal with his denigration, degradation, his total insensitivity, nor the way he can so easily misconstrue the facts because of his lack of insight ever again. Really, he lost and I won. I won my freedom. I felt free for the first time in my life. I'd given him one month. I don't think he even deserved that much time.

My house was pretty clean now without Joe in it, and I began to live again – the right way this time. It was time to banish the old painful memories he'd left behind for me and to replace them with good memories.

Chapter 9
Blindsided

From 2008 to 2014, I spent probably the best seven years of my life. My house was pretty clean now. That adulterous, blind husband who'd caused so much grief and needless and pointless pain and loss was gone out of my life, my mother was being extremely well looked after, I'd removed Jean and Ed who had caused so much trouble for so long with all of their denial and misinterpretation of the facts from my life, I'd somehow survived from the spiritual abuse, I'd done as much healing from all of the abuses as was possible, my physical and mental health was excellent once more, and I didn't have to deal with Grant and his dysfunctional family anymore. I had been so very strong for so very long. By sheer willpower and determination, I had recovered from so many horrendous things that had come at me so very quickly. A lot of damage had been done to me by the above people, though, and I have been left with an enormous number of losses. I have many scars and many, many holes in my heart.

I was having a great time with my son, his wife, and my two grandchildren. During those wonderful years, the children and I had had many sleepovers, I'd taken them to many fun places, I'd put a lot of work into each and every one of their visits, making them joyous and memorable times, and I had just plain loved them. We had such great times together. I would have done anything for my son (Kyle) and his lovely family.

I mentioned that I had given my ex-husband one month – a time I took to deal with all of his antics and to mourn and grieve for those wasted thirty-eight years. The next month, February '08, I went to a church meeting (no, not the one that had set all of this in motion!), and I met a man who very quickly became a huge part of my life. I hadn't planned it that way. I thought that after

Joe, I would never want a man – any man in my life ever again. I was certainly not looking for another man in my life – not after what I'd just been through!

But this man (Ray) pursued me, and we fell into a very special relationship. I was so afraid at first, as my trust had been so betrayed – shattered on all fronts really – but, as time went on, Ray helped me to begin to trust again when I had no conceivable reason to trust anyone ever again. And that was really big for me! He just seemed to believe me and in me, and I desperately needed that. He was so kind and gentle with me, and I desperately needed that. I hadn't experienced that for a very long time. We could talk about so many issues intelligently and openly, and I'd never had that in my marriage. We did so many wonderful, fun-filled things together, and I discovered that second chances in life really can happen. I discovered that a man of substance, integrity, and intelligence could be part of my life, and I really needed that. I will always think of Ray as a gift from God – a very special man whom God placed into my life at this particular time.

Ray gave so much to me – more than he'll ever know. My ex-husband had ignored my gift of music, and now Ray and I would go to music jams. He would strum on his banjo, and I would sing. I also began to play the guitar and accordion again. More importantly, he was a very spiritual man who led me back into the church – a place I thought I would never be a part of again. I knew that I could never fully trust in a church system again, but at least I was able to share in the fellowship of a church environment. Ray shared his family with me! And his family so graciously accepted me as one of them. His family surrounded me with love and understanding, and they supported me as I had never been supported before – an amazing family, like the ones God intended families to be. Boy, after losing two entire families plus a so-called church family, did I ever need that! I will always feel truly blessed with what Ray shared with me in the way of family. He also gave to me his friends, and I'd lost so many friends because of Joe's lack of telling people what had really happened. Ray helped me to restore confidence in myself, helped me to restore my self-esteem, and most important of all, he just simply and completely believed me and in me. My life was so good at that point. At this late stage in my life (I was 68 years old), I finally had a real family surrounding me – one who cared about me!

****

I thought my son could see much of what his father had done to me and to his sister – to all of us, really. He'd been a teenager and then had been away at college when most of that crisis and tragedy had taken place. I'd withheld much information from him about what had really happened during those years because I didn't want to hurt him. He didn't know how bad it really was. I didn't think he needed to know the worst parts. That turned out to be a terrible mistake on my part and was soon to come back to haunt me. It was also going to steal what was left of my family away from me for a time.

****

Then, when my grandchildren were visiting one time, my grandchild was talking about a wedding they'd been to in my town. When she mentioned the name of the bride, I knew that it was my ex-husband and the female from the Maritimes who had called me on 26 Dec '08 (one of his mistresses). This wedding had taken place right in front of me – practically in my backyard, at a place where I had often taken long walks! They could have gotten married two hours away at his sister's place or in Cedar City which was just a few miles away. They could have gotten married down East or wherever they were co-habiting. They could have gotten married anywhere else in the world, but they chose to get married right in front of me. I could have been taking a walk there on that day! I had told some of my friends about the *Nightmare Years* and they were now astounded at the arrogance this man had! Was this done intentionally to humiliate me? The two adulterers had come to the town where I had lived for nearly 50 years. It will always be beyond me to understand their lack of tact and empathy. The arrogance that they displayed in doing this right in front of me was a very blatant act – something I never could have done.

Here we go again! Once again, this was like Joe was saying, "See, look at me. I can do anything I want." And he had. He'd flaunted that wedding right in front of me like I was invisible. I had gotten him out of my life in January 2008. I didn't care that he'd gotten married. I firmly believe that this was purposely done so near me with full intent to hurt me some more and to 'prove that he could do anything he wanted to, whenever he wanted to, and get away with it'. It was very indicative of what he is capable of. Joe had treated me so inhumanely, and now by flaunting this wedding in front of me like that, it was like telling me, "You are a non-person. You don't count. You don't matter." It implied that I am not important, I don't exist, and I am not allowed to have any feelings. After all the suffering I had done at his hand, I was once again invisible.

It shocked the hell right out of me to learn that my son, his wife, and their children had gone to this wedding. They hadn't told me about it – more secrecy and silence and more 'don't tell'! I was completely blindsided. My God, I found out from my little five-year-old grandchild. I'd had to fight with everything I'd had within me to get back what I could of a completely destroyed life, and I had just climbed out of the horribleness: Kayla didn't make it out on time. All the damage he'd done for so long…and yet, here he was as bold and brazen as could be. I just could not believe the audacity of this guy! After all the deception he'd instigated, all the credibility he'd stripped me of by not telling anyone what was happening in our home, and the way he'd just stood silently by, I just couldn't believe his boldness. If anything, he should have come back here shame-faced and full of remorse. Joe does not sit on any pedestal.

****

And this is when I learned that memories of past abuse can be retriggered (no matter how fully you've dealt with all of it), and you can go right back into PTSD again. This was a very shocking turn of events. This was such an obvious display of the entitlement Joe felt. It was also a perfect way to diminishment me some more. I didn't know what to do about this new development. I didn't think Joe could display such a lack of discretion by coming back here ever again. He should be so ashamed of himself.

And here I was – living through all of my past yet again, those old scars and festering wounds being ripped wide open and bleeding all over the place again. Damn it! Damn Joe! Once again, I didn't know what to do with all of this emotional pain – all this hurt that had been retriggered by this ridiculous wedding. How could I possibly go through all of this again and survive?

I didn't think I could go through all of that for the third time. I was so fortunate to have Ray in my life at that time. He didn't just ignore me when I was going back into shock or just leave when I found myself re-dealing with my abusive past again. He is not like Joe was and didn't just leave when the going got rough, even though he didn't understand it all. I had never had this kind of support, and I thank God for it every day. Because of Ray's constant support, I recuperated much more quickly from the PTSD. He just supported me and believed me and in me. That's all I've ever really needed and had never really had. Ray even contacted my doctor. Too bad I hadn't had a real man like Ray in my life back in '94, '95, '96, and '97!

A person has to be mighty careful when they are a part of reopening old, painful, and devastating wounds that had, in my case, taken about fifteen years to heal. When those wounds are ripped open again, as what was happening to me, was I going to have to spend maybe the rest of my life healing from all those painful memories yet again? I was 69 years old at that time. Joe will always be a major trigger for 'remembering'. I was really, really tired of taking the fall for people who have twisted the facts (to their advantage) and caused so much damage to me.

What is it about me? Do I have a sign on my forehead that says, "Feel free to hurt me! I'm waiting for you to come and hurt me! Please, feel free to hurt me!" That's all my life had been about for a very long time. I just could not bear this injustice anymore – not even for Kyle. It hurt me so intensely that my son could go to this wedding after the way his father had damaged my life so badly. We all know that it can be very damaging to a child, no matter what their age is, to hear one parent speak negatively of the other parent, but Joe had done such severe and extensive damage to me. By including Kyle and his family in that sideshow wedding, he'd just gone way too far this time.

It was like I didn't matter at all. That they could go to this wedding knowing that I would most certainly find out about it and yet not tell me about it was extremely hurtful. We'd had such a close, terrific relationship. I thought I had finally gotten rid of all the coverups, secrecy, and silence, but there it was right in front of me again. This was just another cruelty instigated by that ex-husband of mine. It was a terribly, terribly hurtful, and blatant act. By going to this wedding, it said to me (and everyone at the wedding) that what had happened to me, and all around me, was insignificant – not important – and made me look like and feel like a fool.

Everyone at that wedding did not know what Joe had done to me. By going to this wedding, my son and his family were totally discounting what his father had done to me, to his sister, etc. Condoning what Joe did to me was outrageous. I'd spent so many good times with my son and his family, and now I was just blindsided – my feelings not even considered. I felt like Kyle thought his father's feelings were more important than mine. I didn't deserve that! Surely, if anyone at that wedding would have known what Joe's 'lack of action' had done to his first family, they would never have participated in it.

Why would my son now hurt me like this? Humiliate me like this? Put me into this situation? Those seven wonderful years I'd just had ended so suddenly and so shockingly – just like so many other things in my life.

I just couldn't believe that Kyle and his family would intentionally want to hurt me like that, but they did – immeasurably, and it seriously damaged my already limited capacity to trust anyone or them. It felt like they had just spit in my face. That's basically what Joe and his mistress/new wife had done. This was all wrong on so very many levels. I'm not sure what kind of a story Joe had concocted to tell our son, but I guess he'd made it a convincing one. He's very good at misconstruing facts to make it sound good for himself. I've learned that an abuser can present a completely benevolent persona to the outside world. And his new wife? Well, she must have about the same level of intelligence as Joe, having known him for quite a few years, and she obviously falls short of having a good moral standing. Joe had made a great deal of money on those loan assignments, and it's entirely possible that she would have gone along with whatever he wanted to do. Was it about his money? Possibly. Don't know. Don't care. I don't suppose either one of them will ever read the book entitled *Catechism of the Catholic Church* promulgated by Pope John Paul II where it speaks of adultery, divorce, and remarriage and states, *"The remarried spouse is then in a situation of public and permanent adultery…"* His new wife is in the same predicament and holds the same designation.

****

I finally came to the conclusion that Kyle truly didn't know, or understand, what the full extent of his father's actions had really done. It became clear that Kyle and his family were victims of Joe's consistent wrongdoings too. Surely, my son wouldn't hurt me like this. He didn't seem to see the harmful consequences for me as a result of his going to that wedding. It would have been the perfect opportunity for him to tell Joe that he wouldn't hurt his mother by attending. Nevertheless, he had acted in his father's best interests, certainly not in mine. It was abundantly clear that my son and his family didn't have a clue what had really gone on during the *Nightmare Years* and, especially, Joe's lack of action.

****

I began to have a serious talk with myself (I'd had quite a few of those during the past years), and I decided that "I'll be damned if I'm going to just let this slide by without the truth being out there." I realized that I absolutely had to share with Kyle the full story of what had really transpired during those *Nightmare Years*. It was time – past time. It was time for my son to try to grasp the seriousness of his father's lack of action and to understand all the things that I had been dealing with – alone! I was very angry that I should have to do this explaining when I'd already dealt with so many harsh issues.

He just didn't know how rough those years had been. I couldn't believe that Kyle had stood beside a guy who'd totally ignored the disastrous place his sister had been in and who'd treated his mother so insignificantly, thereby setting me up to be so ostracized, demeaned, trivialized, and denigrated. I just couldn't believe that my son would knowingly hurt me like that. Once again, I was just a great big ball of hurt and pain.

I did need to escape for a while, though. I needed to do a whole lot of re-healing. Those scars were wide open and festering once again. I couldn't be near my son and his family for a time. They'd hurt me terribly. I felt myself sinking further and further back into shock as my memories were being retriggered, and I had to deal with all of that abuse – again!

I actually sold my house and moved to another town. Kyle and his family will never know how close I came to moving right out of the country. I came very close to just running away from my crazy, hurtful life. It really ticked me off that I was the one who'd done nothing wrong and had, once more, been set up for more pain! I'd had way more than enough! And I was the one needing the escape!

****

How was I ever going to tell my son about what had really happened to me? How in the world do you tell your child about his grandparents who had so damaged me as a child, but who had been so very good to him? How was I

105

going to tell him about that uncle and aunt who had caused so much pain for my parents and for me? How do you tell a child about a husband (his father) who ignored his mother and his sister when they were crying out for help so desperately? How do you tell a child about a father who doesn't take a wife to a hospital or doctor when it is so needed and walks off and just goes to bed when his wife is laying on a sofa in such excruciating pain and is so traumatized that she can hardly speak…and so much more. How will I ever be able to find the right words to tell him…My God. My God.

****

My son was older now, and I felt that he would have more insight into what had really transpired during the *Nightmare Years* and would, hopefully, begin to understand the reality of what his father's lack of action really did to our family. The truth would be very hard for him to take. But this was not going to just go away until it was fully dealt with.

****

I spent about a year and a half in that other town. While living there, I wrote several letters to my son. I took a huge risk in telling Kyle all those truths. It was one of the hardest things I've ever done. Until he opened his mind and his heart to the truths and recognized the damages done by his father, there was nothing more I could say to him. I couldn't just stand by and have all that had happened to me be minimized anymore. Nor could I have my integrity be trampled on anymore. A guy like Joe should be held accountable for his actions, not be put on any pedestal. It hurt so badly that Kyle and his family had gone to that wedding, condoning the many ways Joe had harmed me so seriously and in front of some of the very people that Joe had estranged me from. God, that hurt.

Hearing these truths about his father (and about all the other matters) must have been very hard and very hurtful for my son, but I was just so done with people playing games with my life. I'm tired of the crazymaking. God knows I've had it for most of my life. All I wanted was a decent family – one I could trust, one that would believe me and in me, one I could count on, one who won't hurt me, one where there would be no more misplaced trust, no betrayals, no secrets and silence, no 'Don't tell her', no second-guessing, and a family that would support 'me' for a change. A real and healthy family is supposed to do things like that. That shouldn't be too much to ask for. Being minimized and trivialized for so long had taken a terrible toll on me. I was so very tired of being a scapegoat.

I told Kyle the absolute truth – all of it – and I just hoped that my son would be able to deal with the reality of all of it. It is very sad that my son now had to deal with all of this. Mine is a very complicated story, but it is a true story. There is an awful lot of anguish and harshness involved in it, and I'll be damned if I will deny any of it.

I told Kyle about all of the horribleness that I had been in the middle of all alone – and how his father had laughed at me, minimized me, etc., etc. I told all. I asked him if he really wanted his children exposed to a man who was capable of causing such damage to our lives, who had damaged his mother and his sister so permanently, and who was a serial adulterer.

If I'd had any idea that my life would turn out to be this circus of craziness, I would never have brought my son into it. I had wanted to give him such a good and happy life. He deserved that. I was so very, very sorry. My heart ached for him as I wrote the truths about his father and all of the other issues. I knew that I was placing a very heavy load on Kyle.

****

I think, initially, Kyle and his wife didn't believe much of what I had written to them. I can't blame them. It's not a nice story. It's a harsh story with so many twists and turns and is hard to believe. We were somewhat estranged for about 1 ½ years, as they digested all of what I'd written and as I healed once more.

****

My son was in a terrible spot. This was his adopted father, which complicated things so much more, for obvious reasons, and was a large part of why I had not previously shared much about what Joe had done to me with him. Kyle had an awful lot of sorting out to do. My son and I were both in terrible places. We were both put in those places by Joe.

I didn't think there was going to be a happy ending for me. I wasn't sure if my son and his wife would believe me. Stories of abuse are so often not believed. I was so afraid that I would lose Kyle and his family. My son had a lot to digest. I only hoped that, one day, he would understand. But he needed to recognize the fact that his father was not who he appeared to be. I thought that anyone with good common sense would see that they'd be far better off without a serial adulterer for a father (not to mention all of the other things he'd done), but Kyle would have to make his own decisions about whether to continue to communicate with Joe or not. It is not up to me to make that decision. It was important, though, for him to know about his father's actions (or lack thereof). Did Kyle really want a guy like Joe around his children?

****

In 2017, I moved back to the town I'd lived in and around for all those years. I was stronger again, and I was ready to try to make things right with my son.

It had taken a few years, but my son did come to terms with all of the information I had written to him. I had always loved my son with all my heart and soul, and I hated that this tension was between us now. Kyle is a highly intelligent and insightful man, and I think he'd spent the time digesting what I'd written to him, thinking back over the years about what he'd seen and heard, sorting out in his mind what the facts really were, and began to see much of the destruction his father had caused. Truth hurts. I knew that this was hurting him. He had to do much mourning and grieving too. And to hear about what his grandparents had done to me must have been terrible for him to hear. My parents had been such good grandparents and had brought so much joy to my children. Kyle had an awful lot to assimilate and deal with, and I was really sorry to put him through all of that, but I just couldn't deal with any falsehoods between us anymore. Truth is truth.

****

I am very pleased that Kyle decided to keep those good memories of his grandparents. He now knows a lot about their childhoods, and he understands how their lives have affected my life. He knows that I have forgiven my parents, and he has forgiven them also. I have a very wise son!

Today, my son and his family and I are as close as we were before Joe came back here to get married, but it took some time to get to that point. He hasn't seen his father for some years, and their relationship will never be the same. It can't be. Joe caused too much damage. I don't think they can fully understand the extensive damages done to me by Kyle's father, but this time – this most important time of all – my son and his family told me that they believed me and in me – such important words. It would have been such a heartbreaker if I'd lost my son – my fourth and last child – as well as all the other people I had lost so very quickly for all those various reasons and so needlessly and pointlessly. It would have been totally unjust and just so dead wrong.

Kyle and his family really hadn't meant to hurt me. They truly hadn't known the full extent of what had transpired all those years ago. We both learned some serious lessons about communication within a family and what withholding information can do. While my intentions had been good initially, I was wrong in not sharing the truth so that Kyle could understand. I hadn't wanted to share all of that horribleness with him, but how could he understand if he didn't know those truths? *I believe that my son will never keep secrets from me again, even if they hurt, and I will never keep secrets from him again, even if they hurt.* We both know how badly secrets can destroy families. A good family does not keep secrets from one another. Tell it like it is, and let the other person deal with it before it causes damage. Do not blindside others by having them find out things the hard way. A person can deal with almost anything if they know what 'the thing' is, but when you don't know…An excellent example of that is the way the church had mishandled the spiritual abuse and what being there did to me. I detest secrets!

Chapter 10
The Church

I have to go back to the starting point of this horrible chain of events, and that leads me right back to the church that I had been a member of all those years ago. Since much of what I've written about began at that church, I need to elaborate more about how I feel about the church and what I have learned.

In Chapter 3, I spoke about 'cleaning my house'. One of the first things I had to sweep out of my house, sadly enough, was that toxic church. After what happened to me (to my entire life) during that horrific chain of events, and to my daughter, as a result, I can't see myself fully trusting in a church again. On 7 February 1997, I wrote a letter of resolution and moved on from the church. It was a lengthy letter in which I shared with them what being in that church at that time had done to my life. The church did not respond to me. I guess I just wasn't important enough. They just left me to suffer, and that is what I did – for many, many years.

When I had been in such a horrible state of health from '95 to '98, Joe had been telling people what 'he' thought they should hear. It is 'me' who suffered the numerous consequences of his actions. The church did the same thing – told the people what 'they' thought the people should hear. 'We/I' suffered the consequences. Whatever happened to good families who didn't keep secrets? Look what it did to me! The damages done to me had only just begun in '94, and they were endless!

When I went to the minister to seek help for my daughter in 1994 and the problems I could see ahead for her if she continued to see this guy, he just sloughed it off by saying, "Well, they're living together anyway, and there's nothing I can do." He offered no help or support whatsoever, and I was very shocked at his response. I had thought that a minister would be the best person to ask for help, but I was wrong. At that point in time, I think there was a very good chance that, with his help, the situation with Grant and my daughter could have been resolved. If I had known what was going on at the church at that time, I was still in a good state of health, and I would have gone to a counselor to get help for my daughter. [For sure, my husband was doing nothing to help.] But I sure didn't get any help from my church. It felt like my daughter, and I didn't count at all. I would learn later on that the minister had 'other things on his mind'.

When I had directed a play in 1993, which was a story about a husband having an affair, the minister accused me of putting the play on to make him look bad. I was stunned! The hierarchy of the church hadn't told us anything about the minister's actions, so I had known nothing of his womanizing at that time. In 1994, I had been kicked out of a meeting that the church hierarchy held because, as I later found out, they were discussing the minister's actions and what was happening in the church. I wasn't allowed to stay and help to make any decisions. Secrecy and silence, and the 'don't talk rule'. Spiritual abuse at its best.

I was to learn that I had gone from one dysfunctional family directly into another. And all those friends I thought I had at the church? Some of them were on the church board and were told not to 'tell anyone'. Heck, I wasn't part of that church family at all. As a result, I still don't trust any of them. Unfortunately, if I see any of them, even after all these years, my mind immediately takes me right back to those horrible *Nightmare Years*. I instantly remember how I was the forgotten one, and I can barely bring myself to say "hello." That church would have to admit that it had seriously betrayed one that it was supposed to serve. All those things that were happening in front of me at that church were triggers for RMR, and the church hierarchy didn't have the insight to see what it could do to one of the congregants – me.

A couple of ladies from the church finally came to give me some support, but it was too late for me. They had no idea that what was happening in the church had reopened old wounds that it would take the rest of my life to deal with and to heal from. They couldn't provide the understanding or the help that I really needed. At that time (about Feb/95), I didn't know what was happening to me. Was I having an emotional breakdown? Was I in shock? I could barely string a sentence together at that time, and I was in such tremendous physical pain. What they supported me through was the emergency stage of repressed memory recovery, and it was a terrifying, ruthless, painful, horrendous road to travel. I lost so much so very quickly. They didn't know this at the time, and neither did I.

This unhealthy church that I had belonged to had not made any provision whatsoever for someone like me in the throes of repressed memory recovery. They handled the situation atrociously. Who specifically gave the order to not tell us that something bad was happening in our church so that we could deal with it like the family they claimed we were? Where did that advice come from? We humble children of God all had the right to know what was happening in our family. What gave them the right to not keep us informed? Why couldn't they just be honest with all of us? Such deception!

The ladies finally told me that the minister had been having numerous affairs with various ladies at the church. Two years later, I was told? After what had been going on in the church had triggered all of these memories for me? A letter finally went out to all congregants stating the minister's actions and saying the words we'd all needed to hear for at least two years – *sexual misconduct.* After the letter was distributed, there were even more problems at the church as people began to digest this and to understand, or to deny, that what the minister did was wrong. There was much disbelief surrounding the minister's multiple affairs with women in the congregation. This is exactly what happens within a family when abuse is disclosed. Each individual has to come to terms with the disclosed abuse in his/her own way. It's like there is an explosion of emotions, and this is indicative of 'all' abuse disclosures. An awful lot more could be said about this, but the most important thing is to 'tell the truth' right away and let the 'family' decipher it! Don't let it fester and cause more destruction! This is what spiritual abuse consists of. Church discipline is not only to be handled by the leaders. It is to be handled by the entire congregation. Jesus said that. I didn't. But I agree with Jesus.

Yes, it was a terrible abuse of the minister's power and a horrible thing to do to his wife and his children. But others got hurt too. I will always believe that I was the one who was the hardest hit. More than the minister, I blame the church hierarchy for handling the situation so terribly and with such a lack of consideration or concern for anyone who had come from abusive pasts. That church hierarchy should have been dealing with the situation from the bottom up, not from the top down. They should have had some professionals available who knew something about abuse standing by. But they did not. Secrecy and silence and that damn 'don't talk' rule is at the route of all abuses, and the hierarchy had certainly done its part in causing an awful lot of pain during their major coverup. What ministers do in God's house and how they behave themselves sets an example for everyone. Ministers are looked upon as about as close to God as one can get because they have taken an oath to do God's work. He/she is like a messenger of God's word and should be faultless or as faultless as a human can be. When this oath is misused, it is spiritual abuse.

And what about these ladies that he'd been involved with? What the minister did was dead wrong, but what those women did was morally wrong also. The women involved with this minister were supposedly so vulnerable and, therefore, easily controlled by the minister. The minister was a charismatic individual. He also was someone with spiritual power and someone who supposedly had moral authority. He represented God, and his actions had gone against what God requires of a minister. I do not believe that there was anyone in that church more vulnerable than I was at that time, and I didn't begin an adulterous affair with anyone. I have a problem with the way only the minister was blamed for the affairs, and the women were 'protected'. In my opinion, they were just as much at fault as he was (they were half of the affair), yet they got help and were protected from the gossip mill. We were not allowed to know their names. They were married women. If they'd taken their marriage vows seriously, were they not also to blame? How about respecting the sacrament of marriage? One lady claimed that the minister showed up at her house late at night and was trying to pursue her. She took that to the church. Why didn't she call the police if he was stalking her?

In one of the books I read, later on, *Restoring the Soul of a Church* by Nancy Myer Hopkins and Mark Laaser, I got a two-line acknowledgment on page 215. It reads: "Make provisions ahead of time for any people who may become aware that they were victims of any kind of sexual abuse." Incestuous emotional abuse and other abuses should have been mentioned there too, but my point is that the presbytery and the church hierarchy weren't even knowledgeable enough about abuse to know that all kinds of abuse can suddenly be triggered. Do people really not realize that incestuous emotional abuse victims and sexual abuse victims suffer similar consequences? All abuse is deplorable! It is all hideous!

If there are multiple other hard issues taking place in a parishioners' life at the same time as this type of church malfunction takes place, it is a recipe for total destruction. I am a perfect example of that. All abuse is evil. Spiritual abuse is like a raping of the soul and takes tremendous healing. Here I was deep in the throes of RMR, trying to deal with my incestuous emotional abuse, a daughter who was in such a terrible place in her life, an out-of-control mother, and, of course, this husband/father who did nothing. And at this terrible time in my life, I found myself trying to deal with spiritual abuse too.

I never did get an apology from the church, I never did get any professional help from that church to help me deal with that RMR, nor did I get any help with my daughter. I/we didn't matter. Oh, there was supposed to be a lady on the presbytery whose expertise was abuse, but she sure didn't pay any attention to me. I didn't hear from her. I got no help from her. I guess I just didn't matter. I was ignored. Help for me should have come from higher up in the church. [I did make the hierarchy aware of what was happening to me: it wasn't hard to see that I was in a bad state of health.] Well, that didn't happen and, as a result, there was major destruction done to me in every single corner of my life. I will never step into that church ever again. I found that church to be every bit as toxic as the toxic parents I'd had.

I am repelled (disgusted) at the way the hierarchy handled what should have been 'a family matter'. They took away my faith in the church and left me all alone to deal with the aftermath, which was so extensive that it has taken me this long to even set it all down on paper. What I have been left with is so much loss that is unrecoverable. It so destructed my spiritual life and left me with such distrust. I think dealing with spiritual abuse is one of the deepest pains a child of God can know. The destructive power of this church has followed me for the past 25 years and may well follow me to my grave. I felt rejected by that church, and I felt degraded. Why not just tell us the truth, and let us handle it? Isn't that what a real family should do?

I guess much later on, there were meetings at the church, and congregants were allowed to express their feelings and so on. But, by that time, I was in the emergency stage of RMR and in such excruciating pain. I was going so deeply into shock, which turned into PTSD. I was simply forgotten. All these years later, I still cannot go near that church. Ministers and church hierarchies are no longer on that pedestal I'd always had them on, that's for sure. For me, there were very, very grievous consequences – tragic consequences that stole my life away. I was the forgotten one – unimportant.

As a child, and even as an adult, I had always felt complete reverence for any church and minister. At the same time, I had also been somewhat afraid of them. I thought that because the ministers were doing God's work, the churches were places of peace and comfort. After attending this church for 14 years, I found out the hard way that this is not always the way it really is. I didn't know then that the power and control that dysfunctional parents hold over their children is the same sort of power and control that dysfunctional churches and ministers hold over their congregations. I think the church has done some wonderful things in some people's lives, but the church – this church in particular – had been nothing but a destructive force in my life. As a result, my enthusiasm for any kind of organized religion is gone. I just cannot resurrect enthusiasm for ministers or churches anymore – not after the many ways that church was so instrumental in damaging my life so totally.

From what I later heard, they glossed over what had really happened there. Me? My daughter? We got no help whatsoever. I was just left alone to suffer and to deal with it all by myself. That lady who told me that it was good that I remembered my childhood abuse? Good Lord! Little does she know! That statement shows what little people know and understand about abuse. She doesn't know a thing about what goes on during the remembering and all the years of healing it takes afterward. And the loss…the pain…the anguish. Oh, how I wish I had never stepped in the door of that church all those years ago.

I no longer expect to hear an apology for what was done to me in that church, nor for how they treated me. I know that they will never admit their wrongdoing. The level of trust I had in them was so betrayed in so many ways. Now I only hold mistrust and skepticism for them. I was much too badly wounded to ever trust in a church community ever again. I will always be suspicious and wary of any religious organization. I feel pity for that church that didn't think I was worth bothering with. I owe them nothing. I still remember so vividly the evil I felt in that church when I went there to seek comfort – the cold.

In the *New Testament of the Bible*, Jesus warns all people and, in particular, religious leaders who made religion a negative and a trial for believers – more like a burden – rather than a positive, comfortable place of unconditional love and acceptance and comfort. Spiritual/religious abuse should be exposed for what it is. There should be no place for fear or secrecy and silence, nor should there ever be the 'no talk' rule. Those things are all some of the first and the most dreaded signs of abuse. For me, that spiritual abuse felt like the raping of my soul. It was necessary for my survival to walk away from that church. And

I did. If they only knew...the emotional scars that I will always carry. I could no longer be close to God in the church. I had to leave that church in order to do all of the extensive healing I had to do. There was no real care or concern or help offered to me by the church, although many of my so-called friends at the church could see how my health was failing. I thought I had done some good things at that church. I thought I had a church family surrounding me. Instead, I felt abandoned and so terribly alone and wounded – spiritually, physically, and emotionally. When I needed love, support, understanding, and help, they were not there for me. And I needed serious help! I felt so rejected by those who should have been there for me, and I had to take a horrific walk through many years – the *Nightmare Years* – alone. I nearly didn't make it through those years. I now have so many scars upon scars, and I have suffered so much neglect, abandonment, misplaced trust, denigration, betrayal, and more, as a result of the chain reaction of what being in that church at that time did to me. I simply didn't matter.

It is sad that church hierarchies seem to feel that we should just trust them, and we are supposed to respect them and honor them as leaders of our faith when, really, they (at least the church I was a part of) were just another dysfunctional family shrouding us in secrets and silence and building so many mistrusts and so much dissension. Really, it should have been so simple. Tell it like it is, share what is going on in the family, and listen to the congregants. Do it now! Not two (or three) years later when so much damage has resulted from all that secrecy and silence. Those very things are what abuse is made of, and I cannot stress that enough. Tell it like it is! Did the church hierarchy really think we were so ignorant that we couldn't deal with the so-called family situation? I believe that was very narcissistic, and they just ignored the fact that they were inflicting such serious wounds by 'not telling'. I do not believe that is the way Jesus would have handled the situation. The hierarchy of that church used their role as spiritual leaders to violate the trust I had in them. I believe they misused their power and control over us, and the results (for me for sure) were catastrophic. I was a very committed believer and a very committed congregant. People like myself are most often vulnerable to spiritual abuse.

In Matthew 23, Jesus is very angry with many of the spiritual leaders, calling them blind guides, hypocrites, and fools. After what I observed in that church, I am of the opinion that nothing has changed. I read in a book somewhere that Jesus spoke repeatedly about the problem of spiritual abuse and exposed and opposed it. He taught the principles that would generate healing from spiritual abuse and bring wholeness once again to the person. Those lessons have not been learned by all churches – not even today.

The thing is that we are to take our children to church, we are to teach them all about the love of God, we are to be good parents, we are to treat one another as we wish to be treated, etc. My teenage son was going to this church at that horrid time. He will never belong to a church again after he saw how things were handled in that church and after he saw what happened to me and to the rest of his family as a result. It is no wonder that so many people – young and old – are either leaving the church or not going to a church at all today. What happened at this church was very instrumental in completely destroying my life, and I am very sure it brought some really big issues up for others in that church. We are likely people who will not fully trust a church again. I cannot. I've tried.

It is very interesting to note here that Catholics have brought into the open much of the abuse that has taken place in the Catholic church. After I escaped from the church, I learned that there were three other nearby churches of the same designation who were dealing with similar situations at the same time as this was happening in the church I'd gone to – not a good record for any church. I tried for many years to find another church that I felt comfortable in. During that time, I learned that there was a lot of abuse happening in other churches as well, but they weren't talking about it. Hmm…just like the church I'd been a member of. I guess there can be abuse in any church. Some churches deal with it, and some churches merely sweep it under the rug, not recognizing the severe damage it can do to an individual's entire life. One has to give the Catholic church a lot of credit for not allowing the secrecy and silence and that 'no talk' rule stop them from at least attempting to reach people like myself who've suffered so greatly and at least apologizing to abused congregants and trying to make the very necessary changes. I never got that kind of help – or any help. Why do we not hear via newspapers, magazines, and books about all of the abuse taking place in Protestant churches?

As I previously noted, in Matthew 23, Jesus displays deep anger at the religious leaders of that day. I can identify with Jesus. I had usually been a person of fairly even temperament and rarely became very angry, but after being in that church from '92 through '94 with those leaders, I felt the same extreme anger Jesus must have felt. The presbytery (the supposed experts) was conducting (unbeknownst to us – the lowly congregation), in their position of power, a coverup that a real church family should have been involved with from the very beginning. The church just left everyone to guess, question, gossip, and on and on. They didn't allow us a chance to vocalize our anger, hurt, pain, or anything else because we didn't know what was happening in 'our family' – secrets and silence and the 'don't tell/don't talk rule' – just like any other dysfunctional family or, in my case, like in an incestuous emotionally abusive family. The minister was accused of abuse of power, but I think the presbytery was also guilty of that.

Allowing such suppression and deception to exist within a church family fosters gossip and is the direct opposite of what the meaning of Christian fellowship should be all about. By being unwilling to share the problems with the church family, conflict, etc., begins and festers like an open wound. That 'no talk rule' implies that certain problems must not be exposed and must be withheld from us meager congregants. Nobody had any idea what was going on, and tensions were growing in all directions. Friendships were ending. As for me? Well…my memories took over, and there was no stopping them. My previous life ended so suddenly. All abuse is evil and causes horrible destruction. I know. I was literally torn apart, and I nearly lost my life. My daughter did. Believe me, I have no praise for the way the church handled itself. Healthy groups thrive on the free flow of information. Problems can be solved, and solutions can be found but not when you are not even told what the problem is. Sick groups of people suffer from confused, defective, or controlled communication. If only I had never stepped inside the door of that church…

I read a lot of books about spiritual abuse during that horrible time. In one book, *Healing Spiritual Abuse* by Ken Blume, it states, "Problems within churches are to be handled by the entire church, not just a select group of individuals." The authors of the other books I read said basically the very same thing. In the New Testament of the Bible, Jesus gives guidance as to how to handle church problems. He teaches that leadership should not be isolated to a hierarchy group but to the whole of the church. He makes it very clear that church concerns are to be handled by the church as a whole, not just by a select group of church leaders. Have all church leaders not learned that?

In my opinion, in the years from '92 thru '94 and likely before and after that time, the church I'd been a member of was not following the path that

Jesus had set out at all. Being a leader of any group is not an easy job, but leading by playing power games, or withholding important information from the whole of the church, is dead wrong.

What eventually was decided to do about the minister was decided by the church presbytery and by a select group of congregants. I knew nothing about what was going on for at least two years. Judgments placed on anyone (in this case an adulterous minister) should have been based on a decision made by all of the congregants as a whole. Is it any wonder then that all this in-church dissension and secrecy was so instrumental in bringing up my RMR? I wonder what it brought up for others? I do realize, especially now, that I am certainly not the only abuse survivor in the world. There are way too many of us.

Healing from spiritual abuse, especially along with all the healing I found myself in the middle of, was astronomical. I felt like my very soul was shattered. What was happening to me was so grievously misunderstood by those who I thought had been my friends. To think that people who claimed to be Christians could treat what was happening to me so very lightly and just leave me to flounder in a place of horrific physical pain, and even worse emotional pain is so unconscionable that I simply have no words for it. What happened to me as a result of what was going on in that church so profoundly, so negatively, so devastatingly, and so completely affected (damaged) my life. For a long time, there was nothing left of my life.

I had had such blind faith and trust in that church. It's all long gone. The way the hierarchy handled things marked the end of my time as a practicing Christian in any church. It's left me lame and crippled for the rest of my life, with so many damages that can never be repaired. It also left me in a place where I have been so grossly denigrated, so neglected, and so ignored. The worst thing that happened to me was that I was stripped of my credibility at a time when I was 100% incapacitated and in such deep shock, was unable to speak, and couldn't stand up for myself. Such wreckage. Such terrible aftermath resulted for me by being a member of that church at that particular time. Rejection. Enormous pain. Unfairness. Rumor. Secrets. Silence. No talk rule. Innuendoes. More pain. Misunderstandings. Demeaning. Belittling. Loss of reputation. Loss of friends. Loss of relatives. Loss of a church family. Loss of a biological family. And so very much more. The loss for me was endless.

And then I read this book entitled *The Power of Suffering* by John MacArthur, Jr. It helped me so much because it was so confirming. It was my support for a time and will always be on my bookshelf beside *The Courage to Heal* and a few other books that had come into my life so miraculously. While I was losing so much and being treated so inhumanely, so unfairly, and so heartlessly – such a vicious attack on my life – this book was my comfort. It led me into tremendous understanding and helped me a great deal in healing from the spiritual abuse, the incestuous emotional abuse, and the spousal abuse. In that book, the author talks about how God tests us through suffering thereby testing the strength of our faith. I believe that my faith is a lot stronger than I had realized. Otherwise, I don't think I would have been so deeply affected by what went on in that church. The author also talks about enduring strength and how God allows this for greater usefulness. I certainly had endured a tremendous amount during the *Nightmare Years*. I began to realize how I did possess tremendous endurance, hard though it was to deal with all those horrid issues that kept coming at me. There were so many reasons why I needed this tremendous endurance that God granted to me when I was dealing with all of those horrendous, tragic, and devastating issues.

In 1 Peter 4:14, Peter speaks about persecution – "you are blessed because the Spirit of glory and of God rests upon you." I was severely tested, and I certainly felt like I was being severely persecuted. It could only have been with the help of God that I have survived. I so very nearly didn't. I think this is a wonderful book. I think everyone should read it. It was tremendous confirmation for me, and I am very grateful to the author.

To be very clear, I do not blame the church for what happened to me in my childhood, but I certainly do not thank the church for the memories. Would those memories have returned at another time? I don't think so. They were so deeply buried in my subconscious. I will never believe that it was a coincidence that I had RMR at that particular time. Churches need to know about the extensive damage that can result to one of their congregants when a church withholds vital information from its congregation and mismanages that information. They need to be held accountable.

I had found myself in a very dysfunctional church at a horrible time in my life. I am not so naïve that I believe all churches are like that church. I'm sure there are many churches that are ministered to by wonderful pastors who carry out their work according to the way God intended them to. Unfortunately, I didn't happen to end up in one of them.

Healing from spiritual abuse has not been an easy thing to do. I wonder how many others have been damaged simply because they happened to belong to a certain church at just the wrong time. I had to rebuild my entire life, and it was only with God's help that I was able to do so. He was my counselor and came to help me in the most miraculous way of all – when no one else did. I survived only by the Grace of God.

Chapter 11
Thou Shalt Honor
Thy Mother and Thy Father

Laurence Stern was an Anglo-Irish novelist and an Anglican cleric. In 1792, he wrote a novel entitled *The Life and Opinions of Tristram Shandy*. In that novel, he states, "Though in one sense, our family was certainly a simple machine, as it consisted of a few wheels, yet there was this much to be said for it, that these wheels were set in motion by so many different springs, and acted one upon the other from such a variety of strange principles and impulses – that though it was a simple machine, it had the honor and advantages of a complex one – and a number of as odd movements within it, as ever were beheld in the inside of a Dutch silk mill." Those words pretty much sum up the story of my life.

****

"Thou shalt honor thy father and thy mother."

"Children, obey your parents in the Lord, for this is right."

When you are so scared of your father and have a mentally handicapped mother whom you can't relate to at all and who couldn't be a good mother because she only had the mind of a young child, those words are exceedingly hard to hear. When you are experiencing the flashbacks, one on top of the other, for so long (as I was doing back in '94 and '95), stealing away your childhood, and when your heart is being ripped out over and over again at the memories, it is extremely hard to even think that you should be honoring these parents. As I turned each page of the book *The Courage to Heal* and read all about myself, the damages that had been done to me, and the almost insurmountable amount of healing that I needed to commit to if I was ever to become whole, I didn't know if I could make it through it all.

When I recognized all the damages these two people had done to me, I asked myself the question, "Did my parents honor me?"

****

My parents had seriously damaged me. That is a fact. But…what about them? Why were they the way they were? What did they come from? I would be very remiss and neglectful even if I didn't make some explanations regarding why my parents ended up being who they became. They are both deceased now and cannot speak for themselves. So, I will share parts of their stories. I am sure they would want me to speak for them. And their lifetime stories could tear your heart out.

****

My Mother

She had always been mentally handicapped. No, I didn't have a mother who taught me things that average mothers did. There was never any quality time with her, no life lessons. How could there be? She was borderline mentally handicapped. Her intelligence level was about that of a seven or eight-year-old, maybe younger. She tried to cook but would usually burn the food, forgot to turn off stove-burners, didn't know how to plan meals but would eat like two working men, and actually was a dangerous individual to be left alone in a home, especially with two small children. Need I say more? She couldn't help it. She was mentally handicapped. It was not her fault. She did and said things that were so out of context and sometimes so very strange. It was not a good place for a child to be, and, as I'd mentioned in Chapter 3, I identified with her. I honestly thought I was also mentally deficient. I left home the minute I turned sixteen. I just couldn't take the chaos, the turmoil, and the fighting anymore. My home life had not been normal at all and had been very abusive. That is all about me.

I learned that what my mother had lived through in her childhood was very similar to what I had lived through in mine and was, in fact, much worse than mine. She lived her entire life with all of those horrible memories of her childhood buried inside of her. Now I understand her unexplainable rages and why she had such serious personality and behavior disorders. It was the only way she had of coping, especially with her limited intelligence. Her married life was not at all good either.

****

Her father's first wife had died, leaving him with three small children to care for. It was only three months later when he married my mother's mother. She brought an illegitimate child to the marriage. Actually, she was five months pregnant when they were married. Together, they had eight more children, making a grand total of twelve children in the home. My mother was the second last born. To say that it was not a good home would be putting it very mildly. From the very beginning, it was not a happy or close family. There were too many variables. The backgrounds of the mixed family were so very different. The illegitimate child (a son) of her mother was described as an excessively angry, aggressive, rebellious, and cruel boy and man. He liked horses but treated them very cruelly. My mother said she was very scared of him. Her parents were always fighting, and her mother was, apparently, not very bright and did many strange things.

My mother spoke of her siblings fighting all the time and treating her very badly, always making fun of her and laughing at her. The only siblings she spoke of with some respect were the three children her father had brought from his first marriage. There were a few of her siblings, in particular, that she spoke of with nothing but hate and disdain in her heart. One of those was the one who (with her daughter) showed up at the nursing home and then at the MHU and had to be denied visitation because of the bad memories the visits brought up, leaving her so distraught and hard to manage. Then there was the brother who sexually abused her from her early childhood until she left the home.

My mother had spoken so often of the barn that her father had built on the farm. All those years later, when she had disclosed to me what had happened in that barn, I wondered if she had tried, in the only way she knew how to tell anyone about that brother sexually abusing her over and over again in that very barn. This brother had married a woman, and they'd had three daughters. It was not a good marriage, and they eventually separated. All three daughters had been married and divorced more than once. Had he molested his daughters also? There was certainly enough talk amongst the relatives concerning it. This man was supposed to have been a very cruel man and did horrible things to animals (beat them) and to people. My mother is a prime example of that! My mother told me that he once tied a horse to a fencepost, would beat it, and then left the animal to starve to death. The story goes that he ended up in a Psychiatric Hospital later in his life – no surprise there.

There were a few things from her childhood that just didn't fit together. As I'd mentioned in Chapter 5, her sister had told me that my mother had had seizures from about the age of two through the age of ten. She would suddenly become still, then flop down on the floor with her hands and all of her body flailing. Apparently, she'd had many of these episodes. Could these have been grand mal seizures, or were they a result of the abuse she was receiving and the only way she had of acting it out? I will never know, and the relatives were all very secretive about all of it. Don't talk. Don't tell. Secrecy and silence. I will never know if my mother was born the way she was or had some brain damage as a result of hitting her head while having what sounds like a seizure and/or got lost in her mind because of all of the abuse she'd sustained.

When I researched her school records, there was not one disclosure of her having had any of those seizures while she attended school. She had gone to school from the age of six (or so) to fourteen. She had spent all of those years in grades 1, 2, and 3. She couldn't learn and was put back into the same grade time and again. When the teachers got tired of her being in the class, they passed her along to the next grade. She never made it past grade 3. She told me that the teachers were all mean to her, and the children made fun of her and laughed at her. From what I could gather, she spent the years from the age of fourteen to eighteen working on the farm with her father. (She did have some good memories of those four years.) When she was eighteen, the farmhouse mysteriously burnt down, and her father left her mother. I don't know whose decision it was for her to go to live with her sister near the city of Norland. I do know that she never wanted to be there.

When my mother spoke of moving to Norland, she spoke of the dairy farm her sister and her husband had, and her memories were of milking all the cows by hand and cleaning the barn all by herself. It sounded like she was a hired hand. She got room and board but no paycheck. She claimed she was treated very badly. I personally didn't know this sister well – only meeting with her (and her husband) a few times. I (and other relatives I've spoken to) would describe her as sarcastic, a know-it-all, snoopy, denigrating, and very, very critical. She and her husband claimed to be such religious people, but their actions, words, and deeds did not speak of truly religious people. There were many stories about how they would cheat people out of money and goods, steal, and were very condemning and critical of others.

My mother had had an atrocious childhood, and she did not have a good life for the three years she lived near Norland. Her entire childhood had been filled with emotional, mental, physical, and sexual abuse, all mixed up with so much chaos, hurt, and fear. She had been such a battered little girl and young woman. She didn't know any better, and she didn't learn anything about being loved. It breaks my heart and makes me so angry to think that she was treated so inhumanely, was never loved for who she was, and was never given the love and care that should have been her birthright.

****

My Father

The story of my father's childhood haunted him for his entire lifetime. There seemed to be a huge void within him that no one and no thing could fill.

His parents had apparently been very happy in their marriage, and they both adored their children (four boys, three girls). Then tragedy came. When my father was two years old, his mother died of the Spanish Influenza after giving birth to her seventh child only a week earlier. His father gave this child to a neighbor to raise, as he had six other very young children to raise and a farm to work. That must have been a very heartbreaking time for him. His mother also died about the same time as his wife did, and his oldest daughter and some of the other children contracted the Influenza also at the same time.

He couldn't manage all the farmwork and the six children (all under the age of nine) by himself. Eight months later, he met and married a woman who brought four children to the marriage. It was not a good union and turned into a very stormy marriage. Too many children, too close in age, and way too many variables. The ages of the children were: 11, 10, 7, 7, 6, 5, 5, 3, 3 and 2. The arrangement didn't work out, as one can imagine. They constantly argued over the children, and two months later, the woman and her children left the home.

Apparently, he went to see her from time to time and tried to get her to come back, but she didn't. Some time after she had left, he went to see her and had supper there. On the way home, he got very sick – was vomiting – and was violently ill by the time he got home. Shortly after 12 midnight, he died. It was a very painful death. The cause of death was strychnine poisoning. There was a suicide note, but there was a strong suspicion that he had not written it, as the writing was not similar to his handwriting. There was a strong suspicion, felt by many, that his wife had administered the fatal dose at suppertime. By whose hand the fatal dose was given was never proven.

What was to become of these six little orphans? My father was only three at the time of his father's death. Nobody seems to know for sure how the six children were distributed to various homes around the farming community near the town of Rutherford. But one thing really strikes the very core of me. These children had all been baptized, and all had sponsors (within a church); yet, none of those sponsors stepped up and followed through with their promise to God to care for the child they had sponsored in the event that their parents died. (Perhaps those sponsors had lost members of their families due to the Spanish Influenza as well.) Remembering how mistrustful of the church I was when I began taking my children to church and not knowing why I felt that way, I have to wonder if my mistrust of religious organizations had begun long ago in having been told about this and seeing how it had affected my father.

The only child who ended up in a good home was the baby, who said she was safe and happy and in a loving home. After her father died, the family adopted her. The other six children were not as fortunate. The people who took the children into their homes didn't want the children to know that they had brothers and sisters, and they wouldn't let them discuss their siblings or their parents. The circumstances surrounding their father's death were withheld from them. They would not take them to their parents' graves and wouldn't allow them to visit with their siblings. The children just knew that there was something really horrible about them that no one would tell them – something which left them feeling as if they were inadequate and unworthy. One boy said that the people who took him in "wouldn't allow him to recognize his siblings at all, and it left him with no family feelings at all."

Most of the children knew they had sisters and brothers who lived nearby, but they were too frightened (even as young adults) to speak to them or to make any sort of contact with them. One of the stories my father used to tell was about when he first learned that he had a brother. He had watched a young boy out working in a field. It is uncanny that this boy looked almost identical to my father, which perhaps had heightened my father's interest in him. (I met this brother when I was about fourteen years old, and I was simply stunned. This man was a replica of my father! They could have been identical twins. Even their mannerisms were the same. How sad that they hadn't grown up together.) Finally, my father snuck over to the field where his brother was working, and they talked about their lives. They made a pact to run away together someday. That never did come to be, unfortunately, and my father got a severe beating (one of many beatings) when he eventually was caught talking to his brother. They never saw each other again until they were adults.

One of the sisters went from place to place doing chores for different people, even at an early age. One other brother was shuffled to a variety of homes, which left him feeling very unwanted. I spoke of my father's beatings. When my father was four years old, he and one sister (after a year of being shuffled here and there) ended up living in the same home. The man died when my father was eight years old. The woman married a man soon after, and that is when many brutal beatings and horrific mental and emotional abuse took place. When my father was somewhere between nine–twelve years old, he worked as a shelf-boy at a store in Rutherford. The owner of the store liked him and wanted to take my dad into his home to live with him permanently. But my father was too afraid of what would happen to him if he told the couple he lived with that he'd had this offer from the storekeeper. My dad turned the kind store owner down out of fear, and he regretted making that decision until the day he died.

The six little orphans had lost both of their parents within two years. They had gone to homes that were very undesirable. They were never adopted and felt like they really didn't belong anywhere. They were left with no sense of family, were separated from their siblings, not allowed to see them, couldn't do any mourning or grieving, were treated badly, and held all of these feelings and emotions inside of them – in fear.

My father carried a great deal of anger inside of himself. He had every right to be angry. I'll recap his life: His mother died when he was two, his baby sister just disappeared soon after, this strange woman and her four children moved into his house (ten children altogether), there was much chaos and arguing, suddenly this strange woman and her four children were gone, within the year his father was either poisoned or committed suicide, he was separated from his other six siblings, he went to live in a few different homes before going to live with the older couple who took him and one of his sisters in, the man died when he was eight, the woman married a man about a year and a half later who brutally beat him daily – hit him with whatever was at hand (a club, fencepost, belt, whip, leather harness, etc.) from the age of eight through about nineteen or twenty (I'm not sure), and verbally and emotionally abused him continuously during that time. The man was cruel to his very core. He worked my father like a grown man. When my father was fourteen, he was fixing a barbed-wire fence. When he was pulling the wire away from a post, a staple came out and landed in his eye. He removed the staple and continued to fix the fence. Was he ever taken to a doctor? I don't know. My father never said so. It is very likely that he was too afraid to tell anyone about it. Needless to say, he lost all vision in that eye permanently. The woman, apparently, was also quite mean. My father finally left that home, bought a small farm in another province, and lived there alone until he was twenty-six. I don't think I have to explain further how damaged this man (my father) was by then. My father's story is such a horrible story of emotional turmoil and such mental and physical abuse that, even as I'm writing this, I feel intense anger at those who were supposed to be responsible for caring for that battered little boy and did not.

He told me that he had a hard time fitting in anywhere. He hadn't any sense of having parents, or family, or being loved. He had never been nurtured or cared for like a child should have been. Toxic parents? He didn't have any parents at all. He'd spent part of his childhood with one of his sisters, but he'd lost his other six siblings and never did get to know them until he was much older. By then, their lives had drifted in such different directions that they never had the sibling closeness that should have been theirs. All of that was lost. They were strangers. The boys, in particular, were so negatively affected. And...their wives and children (me) suffered in various ways – all because of what had been done to them in their childhoods.

Then, when he was visiting with his neighbors one day, he casually mentioned that he was twenty-six years old and was thinking that maybe he should get married and have a family. You have to wonder at this strange coincidence, but as it turned out, the neighbor lady just happened to have a sister (my mother) in another province who she claimed was single, twenty-one, and was a hard worker. She made this lady sound like a good candidate for a wife. The neighbors even offered to take him to Norland to meet her. And that is exactly what they did. When my father first met this lady, he thought she was a little slow in thinking, but he thought that 'it couldn't be that bad'. After all, no one told him about her limited mental capacity. He also thought my mother said some really strange and inappropriate things at various times, but he could have had no idea how devastating her mental health really was, and they did not tell him. The sisters made sure that the three visits my parents had in Norland were very short, which he also thought was very strange. This seems pretty important when one really considers how this took place. When you look back at it, it was like they had found an unsuspecting man to take her off their hands. He told me just before he died that he felt like he'd been set up. I agreed with him.

My Birth Family

My father and my mother were married a very short time later. It was to be a union of two individuals who were so very damaged in so many, many ways – a horrific marriage. It was a disaster, and we all paid. My mother was pregnant when they were married, and it will never be known whether it was by my father or not. I have wondered about that many, many times. Siblings can be very, very different, but my sister and I do not look anything alike, our size is very different, our dispositions are totally different, and our outlooks on life are so different. We are just different in every single way. We never got along when we were children.

****

At the beginning of the marriage, my father thought my mother would/could learn, but she never did. She couldn't grasp the concepts of even the most simplistic of tasks. When my sister was born, my father had to take her to my mother and show her how to breastfeed, show her how to change diapers, and show her how to care for Jean. It was within a year that my father realized what limited mental capacity my mother really had. He tried to teach her how to do things, but she just didn't have the ability to learn most things. I was born two years later. I often wonder how we survived our early childhoods. I do know that I ended up in a hospital once when I was about two. I have memories of being in a crib with bars and was looking out a window. Years later, I tried to get the medical information from that hospital stay, but the hospital had burnt down, and the records had not been saved. I only remember feeling very bad. I will never know why I had been in that hospital.

Years passed. We moved several times. My father kept trying to teach my mother how to do things but to no avail. The house turned into a tumultuous, scary place to be, as I have previously stated. My father tried to tell people about my mother, but they didn't believe him. He took her to doctors a few times, but they only spoke with her for brief times and 'didn't think she was that bad'. No one believed him. After a while, he just covered it up and tried to make the best of it. That was better than trying to explain her to anyone and looking foolish in their eyes. They couldn't see that one had to be with her for days, or weeks, to see how limited her mental abilities really were. Dealing with her was so frustrating, and she could make you boiling mad with some of her antics. She was so unpredictable. It got pretty violent and frightening in that house sometimes. As a result, my parents were both emotionally unavailable most of the time. My mother couldn't be left alone for long because my father never knew what he would find when he got back. As for my mother, she was like a small child trying to live as an adult in an adult world. I will never know how my father managed it all. The years passed, and he just put up with it.

My father had been so very abused in his childhood. I don't think people realized how underconfident he was and how low his self-esteem was. He always tried to put on his happy face when we had company, and he had a wonderful sense of humor. I learned that he was actually a highly intelligent man, but the abuse had stolen away his sense of worthiness. Looking back, I think he didn't believe he deserved any better than what he got. Very sad. My sister and her husband were no help. They tried to cover up my mother's actions too, and they never did understand my father's anger. As I previously mentioned, when he grew older and was beginning to have some health issues, he went to them for help and told them that he couldn't live with her anymore (that she was too hard on him). He wanted/needed their approval and understanding. He'd been living under very adverse conditions for so long. They told him he was crazy for having such thoughts and asked him to leave their house. For their sake, my father stayed in that horrible marriage until the day he died. Jean and Ed's reasoning. "We have to live in this town. We would be too embarrassed. There's nothing much wrong with her; it's you." I think most people would say that it was so totally illogical – ludicrous. Really, it was heartless and cruel. I don't know how they could have left him in that state. My father stayed with my mother because he didn't want to hurt Jean and Ed. Even today, Jean and Ed are both either in tremendous denial or still covering up what somewhere inside they must know to be the truth. Or are they really that blind to all of it? I don't know. I gave up trying to figure them out a long, long time ago.

Yes, my father really damaged me. But, at the same time, we were very close and understood each other. When I was a young child, I had looked up to him and thought he was the greatest dad in the whole world, which is why I felt so completely devastated when I so suddenly remembered the emotional (and some physical) damage he had done to me. There was no one else in that family that I could relate to. We were kindred spirits. We had a special relationship, we thought alike, did things alike, we joked together, laughed together, sang and played the guitar and accordion together, and we worked together. Then, in 1995, to so suddenly have those buried memories resurface and finally have to admit that he had harmed me so badly…it just completely broke me. It felt like my heart had been torn out. I wanted to die. I wanted to cling to those happy memories. There were some. I wanted to stuff those damn bad memories back where they came from, but there wasn't one thing I could do to stop them. I tried.

****

Final Thoughts

I spent a great deal of time with my father after he had his first TIA'S in the summer of 1992 and until the day he died in early 1994. We shared many, many things. I listened to him – really listened – and, as I did, I realized how very much pain he had held inside of himself for his entire lifetime. It was a tremendous honor to hear his most innermost thoughts, and I felt even more honored that he felt he could share those private thoughts with me. I realized that my mother could not care for his medical needs nor provide the emotional support he needed and deserved. I realized that this was a man who had never had anyone who had looked after him or cared about him for his entire life.

Looking back, I realized that nobody could ever have tried harder than he had tried to build a good family and to hold it together. It just couldn't happen. I do not regret the last 1 ½ years of his life that I spent helping him to die in as good a state of mind as was possible – hard as it was. As in my own story, he had no one else in his life who believed him and in him. There was no one else who understood what his childhood had done to him nor what it had been like to live with a woman like my mother.

I asked my father near the end of his life why he had stayed with my mother. He said he felt like he was at such a stalemate. Nobody he tried to talk to about my mother had believed him, and he would feel like a fool. (I now know what that feels like!) Jean and Ed had denied him in his efforts to live separately from my mother, and he felt trapped. It tears at my heart to think that he felt he had to stay in the life he'd found himself in. He deserved so much better than that. My mother had never told him about the sexual abuse, and I don't think he would have dealt very well with learning that she was mentally handicapped. He expressed concern about her future because, as we both knew, she could never make it on her own. I think he was an incredible man. A while before he died, he told me that he didn't know what he would have done without me all those years and called me his Guardian Angel. I guess one could say that placed a lot of responsibility on me, but I do know that I was the only person who ever truly did understand him. There was no one else who had the insight into this man's life – no one. That is very sad. Shortly before he died, we discussed what was going to happen to my mother. One of the things he said was, "You don't know how hard it's going to be for you." I made a promise to him that I would make sure she would be well-looked-after. I have kept that deathbed promise. I didn't know then what it was going to cost me.

****

In the first chapters of this book, I've shared much of what happened to my mother (and to me) after my father died, but I haven't written about what she felt and what she went through with her limited level of understanding. Her caregiver of 50+ years had died, and she didn't have the ability to get along with anyone or understand why she had to go to a Psychiatric Hospital and suffer the stigma of being there. She didn't understand that she had wound up there because of the abuse she had sustained as a child and during her lifetime, paying over and over again for what had been done to her. She walked through the pages of *The Courage to Heal* too. Watching her and trying to help her and do all the right things for her was terrifying, and it nearly tore my heart out. My mother ended up in Psychiatric Hospitals because of abuse, and I hated leaving her there. After what I have witnessed and learned in those Psychiatric Hospitals and the MHU, I would be willing to bet that a very high percentage of all people who live in psychiatric facilities are there because of abuse – all paying for what has been done to them. (I read somewhere that 90–95% of all prison inmates have had very abusive childhoods. I'd be willing to bet that psychiatric facilities show similar statistics.) Many times, even today, the world doesn't place much value on the mentally ill, and they are looked down on, but they are important too, and there is a great deal to be learned from them if one opens their mind. Most of them have an important story to tell, just as my mother did.

Such a pity. Someone's got to love, understand, and stand up for someone like my mother, just as someone had to stand up for my father. That ended up being me, and I don't regret it. What she had gone through in her childhood, and what I saw her going through after my father died, was heart-wrenching. She lived in a sad, painful, angry world during those years. And boy, were those years ever hard on me. I had no outside help whatsoever, as I've mentioned previously. It seemed like a miracle to me when the MHU opened just months before they admitted her – a place where she spent the last seventeen years of her life and the best home she'd ever had, even if she didn't always realize it. She had never been treated so well. The staff who worked on the MHU became her family, and they became my family as well. I finally had some support, and I really, really needed it. I simply cannot give enough credit to the social worker and to the care manager. The staff was all so good to my mother – amazing individuals – all of them.

****

My father had taught me a great deal about real human value and about how the human spirit can be so totally destroyed by so much mental anguish. And what my father had not taught me about real human value and what the human spirit can endure, my mother taught me. My mother died in 2013. I made sure she was buried in peace and with love surrounding her. With all I knew about my parents' lives and with what I feel in my heart is right and just, I could not have left either one of them at the end of their lives, no matter how much damage they had done to me.

I accept that my parents were the best parents they knew how to be. I realized through the years that they loved me as much as they knew how to love anyone. I don't think they knew what love is supposed to be about. (I had the same issue for many years.) They were both born into such terribleness. They were not bad people. As babies, they were not responsible for what they were born into. There was a kindness and a gentleness within both of them. They were good people, but they were tormented souls – so very damaged by abuse. It is so sad that they didn't learn about what being loved means. It is sad for me too because I still associate love with being hurt. I am very selective when I deal with people and extremely selective as to who I actually tell that I love. I long ago had recognized this as generational abuse – again, at its very finest. Generational abuse destroys lives. Look at what it did to me! How many stories similar to mine are there out there?

Yes, I had always been a little parent, but they trusted me when they really couldn't/didn't trust anyone else. They relied on me so heavily because they knew they could trust me and knew that I would do the right thing. Near the end of her life, my mother told me that I was her best friend. Truth be told, I was her only true friend. It was that incredible social worker, that wonderful care manager, and the staff on the MHU who showed her what family was supposed to be all about. They loved her unconditionally, treated her with respect (even during the really rough times when strict discipline was necessary), and provided her with the best family she'd ever had.

****

I have forgiven both of my parents. That forgiveness thing and that blame thing can get really complicated, and it is not easy to work out either of those things. It became easier for me to forgive them more and to blame them less as I began to understand that they were both survivors of abuse also. What a legacy! Coming from the childhoods that they did and living in the homes they did, how could they have ended up being anyone else but who they were? I know that they never intended to hurt me. They did, but they did not do it on purpose. My father would have been horrified if he had known what damages he'd done to me, as my mother would have. I firmly believe they did their best with what they knew, and that's really all any one of us can do, isn't it? Yes, they made me into a 'little parent', but sadly, I realized that I was the only real mother my mother and father had ever known – one who loved them unconditionally – the way God meant it to be – the way He gives it. Maybe that was one of my main purposes in life. It may sound like I'm rationalizing what my parents did to me. I'm not. They stole my life as it should/could have been away from me. When I consider what was done to me in my childhood, I think I'm being pretty generous here. What I'm trying to stress is the importance of uncovering your background to see where that abuse came from so that you can understand how it happened, how it affected you, and ensure that you are not a part of carrying it on.

I have learned that people who abuse most often are acting out a part of their pasts. And their pasts could have been damaged by their parents' pasts and so on. It is sometimes a multi-generational legacy that goes on and on until someone finally gains the knowledge and the courage to stop it. I have stopped this horrible legacy. I am very proud of that. In other words, this behavior was learned generationally. As an adult, and after all the study I have done regarding it, I realize how important it is to piece together the stories from your parents' childhoods so that you can, as in my case, have compassion for what they lived through and, as previously mentioned, find it a little easier to forgive them and to not blame them as much for the damages they didn't know they were inflicting.

I was very reluctant to lose the good memories of my childhood. I had those bad memories buried so deeply within me for so long, and I wanted to keep them buried. It was a tragedy that I had to remember them. But I did. I have had to mourn the loss of my childhood before I could find a place to keep the good memories and replace the bad ones with more good ones. I have done that. I have mourned the loss of that little child who had been so battered and torn in so very many ways. I have mourned and grieved so hard for that inner child – that child who had been so damaged and died a long time ago – that child who had paid for a lifetime for what had been done to her in her childhood. That child is dead now. I have cried and cried for my inner child. I've done all of that now, but it's taken most of my adult life to do that. I had to face all of that anger (Oh boy, I have been angry at times!), I had to do all of that mourning and grieving, and I had to get through all of that enormous pain. I think one of the most important things in being an abuse survivor is not to ever, ever minimize what has been done to you and do not ever let anyone else minimize it either. That happened to me, and it is terribly, terribly hurtful.

Forgiveness? I have come to think that the reason it's so important to forgive is to regain our own emotional freedom and to find peace of mind. God asks us to forgive so that we will also be forgiven. I have had a lot to forgive, and my process is still ongoing.

****

Many years ago, Carl Gustav Jung wrote, "The more intensively the family has stamped its character upon the child, the more {the child} will tend to feel and see its earlier miniature world again in the bigger world of adult life." The family I had been raised in had certainly shaped the way I had viewed my life. That view has changed immeasurably since 1995.

****

Abuse is extremely complicated. It has been a very big job to be healing from incestuous emotional abuse, spiritual abuse, and spousal abuse while dealing with the almost unbearable tragedy (the almost unendurable pain) of the death of my daughter under such horrible circumstances and with all the other crises I've written about – all at one time. So much of this pain and tragedy could have been avoided. For me, it's been like being on a horrendous emotional roller-coaster ride that I just couldn't seem to get off. It's been like a great big jigsaw puzzle with so many rough edges and so many twists and turns with pieces that were so hard to fit into such tight places, and I think it is amazing that I have now put it all together. It was such a chain reaction of so many horrific events, and I've ended up with scar upon scar upon a scar. Some of those scars are still partly open. I don't think they can ever be fully healed. I have wondered why I had to go through all of this and why I was put into all of those horrible places. Well…I just was. God placed me in those places. Who am I to argue with that? He gave me everything I needed in order to deal with all of the many horrid issues that came my way so quickly – hard as it was – and He carried me at times when I was so broken. Physically and emotionally,

I have suffered more than most people can ever imagine. I have lost so very much because of people who put so many roadblocks in front of me and who didn't believe me and in me when I sought help.

After I did most of that emotional healing, I had another really good talk with myself. I was not going to let abuse ruin what was left of my life! No damn way! I was a lot tougher than that! Some very important things had happened to me! I was not going to let any of those people who had harmed me, those who hadn't believed me and in me, and those who had just left me to deal with all those tough issues alone have any power over me anymore. While I was in the emergency stage of RMR, and while I was in the process of healing, I could have made some really bad choices. I could have committed suicide; I could have started drinking or taking drugs (to numb the pain); I could have become depressed forever and ruined lives around me; I even could have lost my mind to insanity, which I felt I'd come perilously close to a time or two. I decided to hang in there, hang in there, hang in there. I could never do any of those things to myself because I could never, ever hurt my children as a result of my bad choices. There was just no way I would let those who hurt me, in the various ways they did, destruct me anymore. No one was ever going to take away my power and control ever, ever again. Why would I allow for anyone to think that I was so weak, and make any one of those bad choices when I'd been so incredibly strong and courageous in dealing with all of those horrendous issues one on top of the other – all by myself? Really, I believe it is 'they' who are the weak ones, who acted in very cowardly ways and used me as an instrument for their inability to comprehend – a scapegoat. It's so much easier to let someone else take all the flack, isn't it?

I was brought back to this world in 1995 in the most powerful and profound way. I was given strength and courage that I didn't know I possessed. I was given the knowledge that allowed me to deal with all of the issues and the perseverance to carry through with what I knew in my heart was right and just. Truly, I was led by God. I have carried some very heavy burdens. But, through all the pain and adversity, I have also learned so very much. When I die, I want to be right with God, and I want to have suffered for all of the right reasons. I don't think I was randomly chosen to be in all of those places by coincidence. I believe God placed me where I was supposed to be. I hope I have found favor with God. It is the most important thing to me. After the NDE in 1995, I was left with knowing that I must share what I'd learned. That is one of the reasons I have written this book.

Chapter 12
Resolution and Moving On

I have had a huge struggle with the issues of trust and forgiveness. They are kind of intertwined. My trust had been completely shattered in so many ways and by so many people. I had to rebuild trust in myself, and in others, one baby step at a time. When you've had as much betrayed trust as I have, it's hard to know where to even begin. Once again, God placed some individuals into my life who were instrumental in helping me learn how to trust again. The key was that they simply believed me and in me. That was the most important thing of all. And they didn't just tell me to "move on, that's in the past, can't you just let it go?" or the worst thing of all, "forget it!" That just isn't possible! No, they accepted me unconditionally; they supported me and allowed me the gift of time to heal. That support was very new to me because I'd never had it before. From that point on, I healed more quickly and actually began to flourish. But that trust did not come easily, nor quickly.

And to ask me to just forgive all of those people who damaged me so badly – neglected me, denigrated me, ignored me, and so much more – would seem to be an unreasonable request. For a very long time, I had to leave all of that forgiveness up to God because I just couldn't do it. It wouldn't have been true forgiveness that came from my heart back then. I was to let people hurt me over and over again, and I was just expected to forgive them? My parents gave me physical life, and because I studied their backgrounds and have come to understand why they were the way they were, I have slowly been able to forgive them. But as I realized that the other people who had hurt me would never apologize to me or understand what they'd really done to me and would never, ever change, I began to see that it was a waste of my time and my energy to hope for something that was so impossible. Therefore, I have not reached a place in my heart yet where I can find full forgiveness for them. Maybe someday.

The Church

I was a victim of spiritual abuse. As a result, I have spent many years healing from the after-effects of that abuse. I am now in a position where I feel compelled to use my voice to speak out about all the damages done to me because I belonged to that church. See Chapter 10.

In sorting out what was happening at that church, it made me dig so deeply into what I believe in and sent me searching through the deepest parts of my soul. In doing so, it dug out those horrid memories that were so deeply, deeply buried in my subconscious. It has cost me almost everything that was important to me. I am now a survivor of spiritual abuse, but it has taken me all of my adult life to become that survivor. Spiritual abuse has sent me away from the church. It has sent my son and his family away from the church. I am only here by the Grace of God. I made a resolution and moved on in February 1997.

I beg the church; I implore the church: "Ephphatha! Be opened." Be honest. Fully disclose everything, and do it as it comes up – not two (or more) years later. Don't employ that 'No Talk Rule'. Do some acts of repentance. Say you are sorry. Don't be a part of allowing for individuals to have wasted lives. Don't let one other individual have to suffer the way I have suffered. Don't allow for any other individual to lose everything that was important to them. Don't be afraid to put the fear of scandal, retaliation, and a culture of clericalism ahead of the protection of vulnerable children and adults (like my children and me).

Out of all the churches in my community, I have to wonder why I chose to attend the one I did. Was it a coincidence? Is it possible that God placed me in that church at that particular time and gave me the strength and courage to speak my truths so that the church might hear what I have learned about spiritual abuse, how it has affected my entire life, and perhaps guide church hierarchies into managing spiritual abuse the right way – the way God intended it to be handled.

Joe

What more can I say about a guy like Joe? He did such extensive damage to me – to his family. Even after all these years, I am dumbfounded at Joe's lack of empathy, lack of insight, and his complete dismissal of what had been happening in his family. By not telling anyone about my state of health, he left me suffering horribly in secrecy and silence. I could never have left anyone in the condition I was in and not done something to help that individual. By not telling anyone, he stole away from me parts that were sacred to me – my integrity, my good reputation, my credibility, stripped me of human dignity, and severely defamed my character. He set me up to be humiliated, criticized, condemned, ostracized and left me with more emotional pain than I should have had to bear. When I was recovering, I tried to tell people what had happened, and they didn't believe me. After all, "he's such a nice guy." "He wouldn't do that." Huh! I had the truth behind me, but that wasn't enough.

In marriage, spouses make some promises before God. "For better and for worse." "In sickness and in health." Joe didn't keep those promises. Of course, he didn't keep a lot of promises. I think I've shared enough about him in the first chapters of this book, but even today, I am still astonished that he could just leave me laying on that sofa in such excruciating pain and just go off to bed like nothing was wrong. It was the act of a person with no conscience at all. My very life was in his hands. I will always consider this as a crime against humanity. At the very least, it was gross negligence. It will always be beyond me to ever understand how he could just leave someone like that. I can understand that he didn't comprehend some of what was going on. Abuse is extremely complicated, but I had given him every opportunity to find out what was happening to me. He ignored it all. He also had had so many opportunities to help in so many ways and had done nothing.

How am I to simply forgive someone who saw me floundering around so very traumatized, so deeply in shock, and in such excruciating physical and emotional pain, begging for help in the only way I could at that time – a man who just left his wife like that and went off on loan assignments and became a serial adulterer? Joe has never shown any remorse whatsoever for his actions (or inactions). Equally unbelievable is the fact that he just left his daughter in that horrible marriage, begging for help at a time when I was in such horrible shape and couldn't provide all the help she needed. He was actually aiding and abetting a very dysfunctional family (Grant's family), and it was at his daughter's detriment. I do not believe the forgiveness for Joe's indiscretions is up to me to give. I simply cannot give it at this time. I believe it is up to him to ask for forgiveness – for himself.

Joe did serious harm to my life and set me up as a terrible scapegoat. He just 'sold me out'. The very best I can do is to accept what he has done to my life and know that I can never change him. His loss, not mine. He is not worthy of me. And I am not going to waste any more of my life – my time and my energy – trying to justify his inactions or trying to figure out what goes on in a mind like his. For my sake, I made a resolution and moved on. I am much better off today for having done so.

Jean and Ed

To me, it is simply incomprehensible that my sister and her husband were so determined to place so many barriers in front of me. From the time my father had his first TIA, they were a problem. From the time Ed had first said, "No" when the doctor had asked if my father was under any stress, and to this day, they have denied that there were any family problems. Somewhere in their minds, Jean and Ed knew there were issues, but they just denied all of them. "They would be too embarrassed." "They had to live in Sherville." Wouldn't it have made a lot more common sense to work together with me and help me to resolve all of the issues surrounding our parents instead of playing with all of our lives? It is because of their selfish pride that my father stayed with my mother during the last years of his life – no reprieve at all. It is because of their selfish pride that I ended up dealing alone with all of the issues concerning our mother, and it is a terrible shame and a discredit to their characters that they didn't tell truths to all of the relatives but covered up the realities, while I actually dealt with the realities. They looked for every possible way to criticize me while I dealt with the horrible reality of what was going on with our mother. It was like they enjoyed undermining me and letting me take the fall – a curious pair who only showed up to cause more grief when so much damage had been done. A strange pair.

When I took on the guardianship of both parents, Jean and Ed were no help at all. They didn't deal with any of my mother's out-of-control behaviors, didn't deal with her yelling and screaming at other residents and staff, and didn't deal with any of the horribleness. They just showed up occasionally to visit and left her all upset and in the hands of the staff and me to calm her down once again. As I previously mentioned, they were finally told not to visit. It is unbelievable that they could not see how mentally ill she really was. Did they really think that 'there is nothing wrong with her' when she'd been in and out of three nursing homes that could not accept her as a permanent resident, into and out of two Psychiatric Hospitals and finally living on a secured MHU? How ridiculous is that?

They hadn't known Grant and his family before my daughter's death and didn't know that he was an alcoholic, nor that my daughter was leaving him with her son, nor how terrible that marriage had been with all the drugs, alcohol, and swearing. I find it rather ironic that Jean hadn't wanted the man, who she claimed was a drunk, to be a pallbearer at her father's funeral, yet here she was befriending an alcoholic. It was so easy to see. All of their actions (along with Grant and his family's actions) seemed to be a very deliberate attempt to discredit and condemn me. Why?

I have learned that it is futile to try to get people to see what they, for whatever reason, cannot see or want to see. Fear? Denial? You can't deal with people who don't deal with reality. Is it possible that Jean has also hidden in her mind what she does not want to know? If so, I hope she can get through the rest of her life without those memories being recovered as mine were. In my opinion, Jean and Ed took the coward's way out, just as Joe had done. Just as Joe had done, they had made sure that I was wrongfully misjudged by everyone, including Grant and his family. It was terrible defamation of my character. Just like Joe, they 'sold me out'. For my sake, I made a resolution and moved on. I am much better off for having done so.

My Relatives

How in the world could I ever explain all of what happened to my relatives? They all seemed to think my mother was such a kind, loving person. They had never seen her other sides. They had visited only occasionally throughout the years, and my parents were both really good actors, making everything seem so 'nice'. Jean and Ed were pretending that my mother was 'just fine'. I tried to tell a few relatives about her behaviors and personality disorders. They didn't seem to believe any of it. They'll never know how horrifying it really was. They weren't dealing with what I was, and Jean and Ed denied that there was much wrong with her.

After a while, I just gave up, realizing that I would get no support or understanding from them. Except for one cousin, I lost all of the relatives, needlessly and pointlessly. They will never know that I had gone way above and beyond what any child should ever have to do for a parent – all in the best interests of my mother.

And, how could I have had a standard funeral for her? How could I ever have written a 'truthful' eulogy for her? Why would I have put myself in the position of being around people who didn't understand what her life had been about, nor what had transpired during the last years of her life?

Being my mother's guardian had cost me an awful lot. It is an awful thing to not be believed, and, therefore, not get any support when you're in the middle of dealing with so many tough issues. I felt like I was being treated like a leper, yet I had the truth behind me. If Jean and Ed had told the truth about our parents and not hidden it, this would not have come to be. For my sake, I had to make a resolution and move on. I am much better off for having done so.

Sean

And then, there is my poor grandson. It just breaks my heart that Sean is in the home that he is in. He will never prosper in that home, nor will he be able to live up to his full potential. How sad for Sean that he will never know how special his mother was. I could have shown him the numerous pictures I have of her, from the day she was born through her childhood and graduation. I could have shown him her wonderful artwork, and I could have told him all about her life 'before Grant'. Sean will miss all of that, and I'm sure will have a huge void within himself similar to the void my father had always had. I consider it a terrible shame and a grave injustice that Grant and his family stole away that birthright from Sean. They stole away some very valuable time from Sean and from me that could have been so positive and so beneficial to Sean. How very, very sad for Sean. Pointless. Needless.

I can only imagine what Sean has had to live through in that house. But to fight Grant and his family again? I want some peace in my life before I die.

I'm so tired of dealing with all of this damn abuse! My life has been so saturated with it. Sean doesn't look healthy anymore. I don't think he knows that there's something so much better out there for him. He is like a loose end for me, though. I can't help but think that there is something I should be doing for him. I don't know if I can find the energy anymore to help him see that there's a way out – there's a better way. I found my way out with God's help. Maybe God will help me find a way to guide Sean as He has guided me. I cannot make a resolution and move on from Sean. I think I have some unfinished business concerning him.

****

That was an enormous amount of loss within a very short period of time – very, very painful. And that is just the way it goes with abuse – you lose and lose and lose. It meant such tremendous emotional suffering and such a lot of mourning and grieving for what should have been. But, in the miraculous way Christ has of guiding us, he has allowed for me to build a whole new life. I now have people surrounding me who support me, love me unconditionally, and treat me with the respect I deserve.

The Finish Line

At Christmastime in 1934, a minister gifted my father with a *King James Version* of the Bible. My father treasured that Bible and read it often. I think there's a very good chance that my father read the following verses from that Bible that I will now share. In 1 Peter 2:20-23, it states, "But if, when ye do well and suffer for it, ye take it patiently, this is acceptable with God. For even hereunto were ye called because Christ also suffered for us, leaving us an example, that ye should follow His steps who did no sin, neither was guile found in His mouth who, when He was reviled, reviled not again; when He suffered, He threatened not but committed Himself to him that judgeth righteously..." In 1 Peter 3:13-17, it states, "And who is he that will harm you, if ye be followers of that which is good? But and if ye suffer for righteousness' sake, happy are ye and be not afraid of their terror, neither be troubled; but sanctify the Lord God in your hearts; and be ready always to give an answer to every man that asketh you a reason of the hope that is in you with meekness and fear. Having a good conscience; that, whereas they speak evil of you, as of evildoers, they may be ashamed that falsely accuse your good conversation in Christ. For it is better, if the will of God be so, that ye suffer for well-doing than for evil-doing."

In other words, there is a 'right suffering' and a 'wrong suffering'. We are asked to endure suffering for all of the right reasons, and we must ensure that our conscience is clear. If we suffer in the name of righteousness, as God requires of us, we are blessed.

When I placed myself in God's hands back in 1995, He led me through all of the sufferings I had to crawl through, and He carried me for a very long time. I believe I have done a lot of 'right suffering'. I have gone on a spiritual journey of gigantic proportions. Today, I feel free. I trusted in the Lord, and he brought me over the finish line.

Coming Full-Circle

My son and his family are the most special part of my life. I was so afraid that I would lose them when I told them the truth about my parents and about Joe, but my son has tremendous insight, and I think after a rough time having to come to terms with his father's actions (or inactions), he was able to think back over the years and see the damages done to all of us. It must have been awful for him to come to terms with hearing about my childhood when he'd had so many good times with his 'funny grandpa' and his grandma. He's come through it, though, and we are as close as we ever were. I'm very fortunate to have my son and his family in my life, and I thank God for them every day. They have told me that they believe me and in me. That's all I've ever needed, and it's all good.

I have had a wonderful and very special relationship with Ray, who has helped me learn how to trust again. He has led me back to the church again. He has shared his family with me, and they have accepted me as a part of their family. They are a good, solid, Christian-based family. I'm so grateful that they are in my life. Many of Ray's friends became my friends, so I have a great abundance of friends again. And, most important of all, Ray believes me and in me. I feel very cherished and very loved by him. I truly believe that God placed Ray in my life in February 2008. Every day, I thank God for Ray and his family.

I have rebuilt my life from the smatterings of what had been left of my old life, and I have emerged whole. It has taken one-third of my life and has been a long, hard run. I know that the scars will always be there ready to be reopened at certain times (as when Joe came back to flaunt his marriage to his adulterous wife in front of me), but for the most part, even the scars have smoothened. I don't need to be compliant and smooth things over for Joe, or for anyone, anymore. I will never be used as a scapegoat because of other people's ignorance ever again. I am no longer shackled to the pain of my past, nor do I live in the dark shadows of abuse. All of the dysfunctional people that I had dealt with are gone. I am not that shattered, broken, and the oppressed person I once was. My family of the past is gone, and I am not a hostage to that past. I will never allow anyone to take power and control over me ever again. I had an 18-in. X 24-in. X 12-in high box full of papers dating back to 1995, when I first started writing down what was happening to me and all around me. When I was working on the last draft of this book, I ceremoniously burnt all of the papers in Ray's fireplace. It was very cathartic (and healing) to watch my past life turning to ashes as I began to dwell on the new life I now find myself in. It had taken about twenty-five years.

It's very nice to be at peace with the world. It's very nice to feel peace in my heart. So you see, I feel very blessed. My life is going to end well. I have come full-circle.

Thanks be to God.

Epilogue

Why am I sharing my story now? After I'd had that NDE, I was left with knowing that writing this book and telling my story was one of the things I was called to do. It was time. It was now time for me to fulfill that obligation – that strong request – that has lingered in my mind and followed me for all of these years. It seems that God has set this time for me to share my words with those who may need to hear them.

The words have not flowed out of me. Writing this book has been very hard for me to do because of the content. I have spent one-third of my life healing from abuse. Abuse took my daughter and grandson away because I couldn't reach them on time. Abuse stole parts of my life that can not ever be replaced.

I sincerely hope and pray that reading this book will help to affirm and/or support someone right now who has also had to climb his/her way through whatever tragedy, abuse, or other damages that have been done to him/her. I hope it will relay the message that we can be strong enough, we are good enough, we are resilient enough, we can find the courage (no matter what), and we can overcome almost anything that has been done to us. I know this is true because I have been able to survive under some pretty formidable odds. Sadly, there are way too many individuals with stories out there similar to mine.

****

My childhood is definitely not comparable to Truddi Chase's devastating, ruthless, and almost unimaginable childhood. There were unspeakable and heinous acts of violence – crimes of humanity – that were done to her in her childhood. Reading her story is chilling, and I think it's one of the very worst examples of what abuse can do to an individual. I don't think there are words to adequately describe the many horrors she lived through. I think that it is amazing that she survived at all. It is no wonder that the original Truddi sleeps.

But there are reflections of Truddi's life in certain areas of my life. Reading her book had teased my memory. When I read her book (*When Rabbit Howls*), it was like an awakening of something in my psyche, or a premonition, that I was hiding something too. Somehow I understood her need to incorporate the Troops, and somehow I understood her fear and the terror. I had remembered almost nothing of my childhood, always thinking that I wasn't very bright like my mother. I had blanked most of my childhood out – buried it – a vacuum – few memories of it – just as Truddi had. I had left home at the age of sixteen, about the same age Truddi had. When I had the RMR, I think I'd become dangerously close to completely separating from reality and being lost forever. In the emergency stage, I had fought with everything I had within me to maintain my sanity, until that time on the sofa in 1995 when I could not fight anymore. In the book *When Rabbit Howls, Dr. Robert A. Phillips Jr., (Stanley)* talks about the human mind. He states, "...minds that I can only call 'wondrous'... do survive atrocities without falling prey to insanity." Believe me, I feel extremely fortunate to have overcome all of those obstacles that were put before me so quickly.

It occurs to me that perhaps RMR is outside the scope of what many individuals can understand, just as MPD (multiple personality disorder) is. Believe me, it is very real. It is very terrifying. Unfortunately, so many individuals cannot seem to understand how the human mind reacts to abuse. Many times, when we attempt to tell someone what has happened to us and how it has affected us, we are ostracized, criticized, and looked at as if we are crazy. As a result, that makes us hang on to the secrecy surrounding our abuse.

I have been robbed of a lot. I had watched my life crumble away, one piece at a time. When the recognition of abuse hit me, it hit hard. It invaded my entire life, and I was forced to deal with and heal from a variety of abuses coming at me within a very short time. I have had more than my share of the darkest moments when I felt absolutely powerless, worthless, and empty. I am definite proof that one can heal from all abuses if one is determined enough. It takes a load of strength and courage though. It is not at all easy. The road is extremely rough. All abuse is evil. It has changed my life irrevocably. "A fascinating story," that psychiatrist said so long ago, but it is my story, and I can guarantee you that it is not anything near fascinating. It could have been yet another story of another wasted life. It very nearly was.

I survived only because of God's grace and with His love and His guidance. He came to me so personally, and I feel very humble about that – that He cared so much. I know that when there is no one else, God will always be there. All we have to do is ask Him. He showed me how much He loved me and how much He cared about me. He was truly my rock, my refuge, and my ever-present help during all of those *Nightmare Years*. When I had been so broken and my life had hung in such a delicate balance, the strength to overcome all those obstacles had come from Christ Himself. The Lord was, indeed, my counselor. Only Christ could have given me the strength and courage to have survived from all of the things I did. Only Christ could have given me the knowledge to have dealt with all the atrocious issues I did. Only Christ could have given me the courage to share my sad, hurtful story. Only Christ.

When one has been led by the Holy Spirit, as I believe I was, and when you get to the end of all the pain and tragedy, some really special and wonderful things can happen. I now have a new and very peaceful and full life. I feel very blessed to have had my walk with God and that glimpse of heaven, and I thank Him for the gift of this new life every day.

I am nearing the end of my life now, and I know that there will be some people who won't be able to comprehend or believe some of the things I have written about, but that doesn't bother me anymore because while my story may not be believed, I know that everything I have disclosed is true, and that is what is important.

I implore you to take a really close look at how you're treating one another and, especially, how you're treating your children because, as you can see by reading my story, what you do to them, how you act around them, what you say to them and how you say it will affect them for the rest of their lives. I am solid proof of that.

I was an abuse victim. There are way too many of us. We could be walking down the street beside you. You wouldn't know that. You can't see the pain within us. We look so normal. We are normal. It's just that what we've experienced is sometimes far beyond what is considered normal. Today, I am an abuse survivor. I have fought very hard for a very long time for that distinction.

I leave you with one question: Do you also have to clean your house?

As a matter of interest:

90–95% of prisoners were abused in their childhoods.

A high number of residents live in Psychiatric Hospitals or on Mental Health Units as a result of abuse (My mother was one of them). Studies consistently confirm a 50–80% prevalence rate of sexual and physical abuse among persons who later require diagnosis of mental illness (Breyer, 1987; Beck & Van der Kolk, 1987; Rose, et al, 1992; Craine, et al, 1988; Stefan, 1996).

90% of abuse survivors have depressive disorders as a result of abuse.

85% of homeless people have a history of abuse.

85% of abuse survivors have a drug/alcohol addiction.

90% of abuse survivors have eating disorders.

75% of survivors have considered suicide (40% – attempted/15% – succeeded).

Suggested Reading

Truddi Chase/Introduction and Epilogue by Robert A. Phillips, Jr., Ph.D. *When Rabbit Howls.* Jove Publications, Inc./E. P. Dutton, a division of NAL Penguin, Inc./The Berkley Publishing Group, New York, New York, 1987.

Ellen Bass and Laura Davis. *The Courage to Heal.* HarperCollins Publishers, Inc., New York, NY, 1994.

Dr. Susan Forward. *Toxic Parents.* Bantam Books, a division of Bantam Doubleday Dell Publishing Group, Inc., New York, New York, 1990.

Beverly Engel, M.F.C.C. *The Emotionally Abused Woman.* Ballantine Books, a division of Random House, Inc., New York, and distributed in Canada by Random House of Canada, Limited, Toronto, 1990.

Beverly Engel, M.F.C.C. *Encouragements for The Emotionally Abused Woman.* Ballantine Books, a division of Random House, Inc., New York, and distributed in Canada by Random House of Canada, Limited, Toronto, 1993.

Patricia Evans. *Verbal Abuse Survivors Speak Out.* Bob Adams, Inc., Holbrook, Ma, 1993.

Stephen Seamands. *Wounds That Heal.* InterVarsity Press, Downers Grove, IL, 2003.

John Bradshaw. *Healing The Shame That Binds You.* Health Communications, Inc., Deerfield Beach, FL, 2005.

Aphrodite Matsakis, Ph.D. *I Can't Get Over It.* New Harbinger Publications, Inc., Oakland, CA, 1996.

Cynthia Monahon. *Children And Trauma.* Lexington Books, New York, 1993.

Frank Parkinson. *Post-Trauma Stress.* Fisher Books, Tucson, Arizona, 1993.

Jenny Fransen, R.N. and I. Jon Russell, M.D., Ph.D. *The Fibromyalgia Help Book.* Smith House Press, Saint Paul, MN., 1996.

John MacArthur, R.C. Sproul, Joel Beeke, John Gerstner, and John Armstrong. *Justification by Faith Alone.* Soli Deo Gloria Publications, Grand Rapids, Michigan, 1995.

Melvin Morse, M.D., and Paul Perry. *Parting Visions.* Villard Books, a division of Random House Inc., New York/ Random House of Canada, Ltd., Toronto, 1994.

Tom Harpur. *Life After Death.* McClelland & Stewart, Inc. Toronto, Ont., Canada, 1991.

Charlie Walton. *When There Are No Words.* Pathfinder Publishing of California, Ventura, CA, 1996.

Henri Nouwen (compiled and edited by Timothy Jones). *Turn My Mourning Into Dancing.* W Publishing Group, a division of Thomas Nelson, Inc., Nashville, TN, 2001.

Mary Ann Froehlich. *An Early Journey Home.* Discovery House Publishers, Grand Rapids, Michigan, 2000.

Maggie Callanan and Patricia Kelley. *Final Gifts.* Bantam Doubleday Dell Publishing Group, Inc./Simon & Schuster, New York, NY, 1997.

Alexander Lowen, M.D. *Narcissism.* Touchstone/Simon & Shuster, Inc., New York, NY, 1997.

Catechism of the Catholic Church. Promulgated by Pope John Paul II.

Holy Bible – *King James Version*. The John C. Winston Co., Chicago, Philadelphia, Toronto.

Holy Bible – *New King James Version*. Thomas Nelson, Inc., 1992.

Nancy Myer Hopkins and Mark Laasor. *Restoring the Soul of a Church*. The Liturgical Press, Collegeville, Minnesota, 1995.

Ken Blue. *Healing Spiritual Abuse*. InterVarsity Christian Fellowship, Downers Grove, IL, 1993.

Stephen Arterburn & Jack Felton. *Toxic Faith*. Random House, Inc., Colorado Springs, Colorado, 2001.

Keith Wright, DMin. *Religious Abuse*. Northstone Publishing, Kelowna, B.C, Canada, 2001.

Thomas C. Reeves. *The Empty Church*. Touchstone/Simon & Schuster, New York, NY, 1998.

John MacArthur, Jr. *The Power of Suffering*. Victor Books. Wheaton, IL, U.S.A., 1995.

Joyce Meyer. *Beauty for Ashes*. Harrison House, Inc., Tulsa, Oklahoma, 1994.

Billy Graham. *Peace With God*. Word Publishing, Vancouver, B.C., Canada, 1984.

CPSIA information can be obtained
at www.ICGtesting.com
Printed in the USA
LVHW050321160523
747056LV00030B/13

9 781685 6224